Earth Angel Tools

A Journey of Spiritual Awakening

LEA BETH LaDUE

Earth Angel Tools

Copyright © 2025 Lea Beth LaDue

ALL RIGHTS RESERVED. This book contains material protected under International and Federal Copyright Laws and Treaties. Any unauthorized reprint or use of this material is prohibited. No part of this book may be reproduced or transmitted in any form or by any means, electronic or mechanical, including photocopying, recording, or by any information storage and retrieval system, without express written permission from the author/publisher.

ISBN: 979-8-89079-333-1 (paperback)
ISBN: 979-8-89079-334-8 (ebook)

Dedication

This book is dedicated to all the Awakening Spiritual Seekers who shine their Beautiful Light out into the world. Believe – you ARE making a difference.

Acknowledgments

There are so very many people I wish to acknowledge for showing up in my life at just the right time. You have all had a profound influence on my spiritual growth and evolution.

The very first person I want to acknowledge and thank is my beloved husband, Matthew Barker. He believed in me when I didn't believe in myself or my "worthiness" to bring this work into the world. He encouraged me and was one of my best cheerleaders! Thank you is not really adequate, but it is what I have. Thanks for showing up in my life, Sweetheart!

My darling sister, Jana Lynne Ahlers, who has been my spiritual playmate and safe person for so long! I cannot thank you enough for your love and support.

My son, Marc Welliver, and granddaughter, Bloom Welliver, have both been so supportive and loving – sometimes rolling their eyes, too.

I also owe a deep debt of gratitude to Tom Bird, Flavious Richardson, Andrrea Hess, Betsy Coffman, Saari Sedillo, Alina Vincent, and Carol Ann DeSimine for their help, guidance and expertise.

I would also like to thank my parents – George and Ruth Jurhee Bloom, my grandmother – Kate Bloom for showing up exactly as I needed them to. Much love to you.

I give appreciation and thanks to Lee Welliver, Jim LaDue and Jerry Schroeder for teaching me what love is and how to have boundaries as well. Thank you from the bottom of my heart.

I would like to thank all of my Angel Dreamers. These are the people who have done spiritual transformational work with me over the last 15 years. You are the best! I am so honored to have the privilege of working with you while you are doing your own spiritual growth.

I would be remiss if I did not let all of the animal companions I have had over the years know how profound their unconditional love meant and means to me. My present fur-babies are Katy and Bo. Love you so very much.

Table of Contents

Intro: Why I wrote this Book ix
Chapter 1:   Welcome to Earth Angel Tools 1
Chapter 2:   Growing Up and Finding My Own Path 5
Chapter 3:   Coming Out of the Spiritual Closet 9
Chapter 4:   We are Energy Beings and Have a
             Spiritual Anatomy 11
Chapter 5:   Wear Your OWN Energy 17
Chapter 6:   Intro to Spiritual Tools — 20
             Pendulum. 20
             Oracle Cards/ Angel Cards/ Tarot Cards 25
             Soul Tribe / Spiritual Support Group 27
             Psychics: Going to Them 28
             Learning to Channel 29
Chapter 7:   Energetic Property Clearings. My Story 32
Chapter 8:   How to do a Property Clearing & Why. 37
Chapter 9:   Energetic Protection. 45

Chapter 10:	What Does It Mean to be an Earth Angel?	47
Chapter 11:	Soul Shifting?	50
Chapter 12:	Past Lives and Past-Life Regressions	52
Chapter 13:	Messages from Heaven	55
Chapter 14:	Stepping into my Own Spiritual Authority	58
Chapter 15:	What are the Akashic Records?	61
Chapter 16:	Energetic Healing	66
Chapter 17:	More Tools for Your Toolkit	70
	Dancing / Singing / Connecting with Music	70
	Gratitude Journal	71
	Books / Book Stores	72
	Love	73
	Driving in Your Car	73
	Being Out in Nature	74
	Crystals	74
Chapter 18:	Your Own Specific Owner's Manual	76
Chapter 19:	Jim's Journey and Transition	78
Chapter 20:	More Energy Healing	81
Chapter 21:	Your Spiritual Staff and How to Connect with Them	84
Chapter 22:	More Tools	91
	Body of Proof (Journaling Your Spiritual Experiences)	91
	What If Game (or Let's Pretend)	92
Chapter 23:	Ghost Busting	94
Chapter 24:	Connecting with Departed Loved Ones	97
Chapter 25:	I See Dead People	99
Chapter 26:	Heeding the Call to be an Earth Angel	101
Chapter 27:	What Next?	104

Intro: Why I wrote this Book...

The reason I felt I had to write this book is that I want each and every one of you to know that you are loved beyond comprehension and that you are honored and valued for being on the Earth Plane at this time. This is a time of awakening to who we really are and who we are meant to be as a way of combining our soul with the physical expression of us. We truly are ascending into our Godhood. Each of us is a piece of God and we have the ability to lift up the Earth Experience to express our divine nature. The first step starts with you. You can only work on your own spiritual development. You cannot do it for anyone else. However, the others in your life will see the shining example you are by creating and expressing your Divinity here on Earth. So go out and be the best possible version of yourself! You can change the world by changing yourself.

CHAPTER 1
Welcome to Earth Angel Tools

Are you ready to find more meaning and purpose in your life? Are you feeling that you are missing out on a deeper meaning and more soul satisfaction, but you don't know what it is or what to do to find it? Are you feeling the call to be more spiritual and to incorporate more spirituality into your life? You aren't sure what to do next.

More than likely, you are hearing and feeling your soul calling to you to be more of who you really are. You are a Magnificent Divine Being who is having a human experience on Earth at this time, but you are yearning for a way to communicate with your Guides, Angels, Your Own Higher Self — as well as God! The difficulty is that our Earth Plane energy is dense and heavy compared to soul-level energy. All spiritual messages or communications are feathery soft and subtle so they can be difficult to detect, much less interpret!

The primary reason I felt compelled to write this book is that we all need to find our own set of spiritual tools. There truly are many different tools that can help us communicate directly with our Higher Self/Guides/Angels/Departed Loved Ones/Ascended Masters and Teachers/ Fantastical Creatures and even directly with God/Source/All That Is.

Just as we each have our own soul-level gifts, we also resonate with different spiritual tools. What are some of these spiritual tools? Intuition, Meditation, Emotions, Journaling, Dreams and Dream Journals, Books, Crystals, Space Clearing, Psychic Readings, Angel Cards/ Oracle Cards/ Tarot Cards, Pendulum Dowsing, Channeling, Past-Life Regressions and for those of you who are really serious about doing Transformational Spiritual work – Soul Realignment Healing Work. We will be talking about these throughout this book.

You and I were created to be an amazing blend of human and spiritual beings. We are especially being called to integrate more and more of our Divine Soul Nature into our amazing Human expression. We are all finally waking up to this! Our lives were always meant to be easy and joyful rather than difficult and painful. Since Earth is a Free Will zone (we each have free will and choice), many of us have unfortunately forgotten the easy and joyful part of our journey. So, part of our calling at this time is to do a course correction and incorporate the WHOLE of us into this physical experience. There really IS magic! It's just not what we have imagined in our current culture. (It's actually even better!)

Each of us is truly the powerful creator of our own experience, based on the choices (actions, not daydreams or wishes) that we make. These choices can be the major choices, but they are more frequently the small, everyday decisions and actions we take. These are cumulative and can create massive changes over time. And the time can be much quicker than you might expect! The quality of your choices literally determines the quality of your life. Your job is to make choices that align with who you truly are at soul level.

Now for the confusing part: there is not one set of choices for everyone; no "One Size Fits All." You must discover what choices are positive or in alignment for YOU! You are a unique individual and must find what works for you. The example given by Esther Hicks in the book <u>Ask and It Is Given</u> illustrates this very clearly.

If you are in alignment with who you are at soul level, it is much like pointing your boat downstream and paddling with the current. Not only do you benefit from your own efforts, but the Universe is also able to give you a big boost. Most of us, however, tend to believe we should "work hard" at whatever we do and find ourselves paddling upstream. Not only are we working quite hard, but we are also fighting against the current of who we really are, so the Universe cannot help us until we quit paddling upstream and turn in the downstream direction.

We each have lived multiple lives, but this life is an especially important one since we are truly rebirthing what it means to be human. So, take a deep breath and start expressing your Divinity, along with your humanity! You are magnificent! You are also psychic! There is much more to you than your human body. Don't get me wrong – your physical body is truly magnificent and amazing, but it is only the tip of the iceberg. You are an immortal soul who incarnated into this Earth plane at this time to create different types of experiences. Remember, YOU chose this lifetime and these experiences. The awesome news is that if you don't like what you have powerfully created, you can change your circumstances by changing your choices. I know that it may seem like you are stuck where you are – I've certainly been there! (More times than I would like to admit!) But know this – you ALWAYS have choices and can create different results. You are much more powerful than you think! In fact, I now call our Divine Soul Gifts by the term *Spiritual Superpowers*!

I know that I will be presenting you with a great deal of material in this book, which can seem a bit (or a lot) daunting. I want you to know how very much I believe in you and your own innate – perhaps somewhat dormant – abilities. When I say you are a Divine Being, I am not just using a catchy little "New Age" saying. I really mean it down to the depths of my soul! I want you to realize that you really are a Rock Star or a Superhero in your own way. Only you know how you want to express it but let me absolutely assure you that you DO HAVE IT!

Use this book and workbook/playbook as a steppingstone to help you find your own brilliance! Yes, I said brilliance! You are quite literally brilliant in your own unique gifts and talents. Do not pooh-pooh your own abilities, thinking that if you can do them, anyone can do them. This is not true! Learn to be your own best friend, supporter, ally, and cheerleader. You can do it! I am so proud of you for taking this step forward, which allows you to invest in your own positive potential. Once you start doing this, your options and life will open in ways you cannot imagine right now. The journey of 1,000 miles starts with the first step. Congrats on taking that step today!

CHAPTER 2

Growing Up and Finding My Own Path

Who am I? I am no one special and yet I am extremely special at the same time. I have had spiritual or psychic experiences all my life, but because they were happening to me and felt "normal" I would tend to discount them. In my mind these things would be exactly what anyone else would experience in their lives. I am here to tell you right now, do not pooh-pooh these experiences or think that everyone can do what you do. Each of us has unique gifts. Our unique gifts are our specific soul-level gifts as well as our own body, feelings, knowingness and energy field through which we experience our Divinity as well as our Humanity.

My journey has been a long one with lots of roadblocks, speedbumps, and challenges along the way. I always knew there was more to me than just the physical form. I just didn't know how to express it. I was raised Presbyterian in a lovely, small town in southwest Oklahoma. Hobart had a population of less than 5,000 and was a great place to grow up although it didn't always seem like it at the time. I knew there were times that I felt very connected to God and my angels when I was in church when I was a child and a teenager.

I had the opportunity to witness the true faith in action with one of the most spiritual, loving men I ever knew. His name was Jerry Hilton, and he was the minister at our church for several years. Unfortunately, not as long as I would have liked. He was a true man of God and someone who walked his talk. I appreciated how congruent he was, even though I did not know what that meant at the time. He was down-to-earth and yet profoundly spiritual. I am so honored to have crossed paths with him. Even though I never saw him again after he left Hobart when I was 15 or 16 years old, he stood as a role model of how to combine spirituality with being fully present in the physical.

One of the most significant things that happened to me when I was in my late teens was being introduced to the concept of reincarnation. It had always seemed so unfair to me that in traditional religion you only had one lifetime to "get it right" or else you were condemned to hell. Well, what about babies or young children who died early in life? What about all the other things that happened in life? I cannot tell you what an "aha" moment it was when I first heard about reincarnation! It just resonated so deeply in my soul that it was like a huge piece of the puzzle falling into place! Wow! It answered so many of my questions and feelings of unfairness.

Whenever something resonates at a deep soul level for you when you hear it for the first time, it is one of your "biggies." This was one of my real biggies! I was completely blown away and looked for everything I could find about reincarnation! I also really, really wanted to remember some of my past lives. There is a thing called Divine Timing in our universe, however, and it was not meant to be that I remember any of my past lives at that time. There were no effective ways for me to do past-life regressions then, and I was extremely disappointed that I could not recall any, even though I knew in my soul with 100% conviction that I had had many lives before. "Knowing" this helped me really move forward on my life path. It caused me to seek out all sorts of avenues in my thirst for knowledge. And even though my past lives did not come to me until later (which I will share later in this book), I learned and studied a wide variety of "New Age" ideas even though they were not called that at that particular time.

As I was growing up, I was acutely aware that there seemed to be a real mind-body connection between illnesses and diseases. I witnessed this directly with my mother. She was a (mostly) lovely person by day, but she was fundamentally unhappy with her life, and she was an alcoholic by night. This was not a pretty situation for me, to say the least. I saw her medicate and stuff her feelings with alcohol. I also saw her health deteriorate until she passed away at the early age of 53 from pancreatic cancer. Her self-destructive behavior and her lack of self-care caused all her health issues. By the time I was out of the house, I could really see how life choices correlated to health issues. It became a real passion of mine to find corroboration. There was not a great deal of information available to me at that time since it was the early 70's. I was also a little busy since I was going to college, getting married, and having a baby. It is interesting how staying busy can temporarily keep you from confronting the elephant under the living room rug, but it is what I did. Being a champion enabler, I thought my life was going really well, although it always felt as though something was missing or that I was not really "real." At that time, I always felt like I was playing a role in my life. It was a role about me, but it wasn't the real me. I felt that if I ever let anyone see the real me, they wouldn't love me or approve of me. (And when you come from any sort of dysfunctional family, these two things are the same!)

My mother's passing was sad and difficult. She endured a great deal of pain, so when she did pass, it was a relief. She was not an easy person to live with or be around. I have learned in the years since her passing that she truly helped me on my path by giving me something to push against. She did not choose an easy path, but I am now extremely grateful to her for agreeing to play her role. Did I feel that way while I was growing up? Absolutely not! But she did force me to really work on healing myself and the wounds I had from my dysfunctional childhood. I have done many, many sessions of forgiveness work so I could clear and cleanse my body and my energy so I would not continue to be the walking wounded. Thank you, Ruth Jurhee, for being one of my very best teachers and for helping me really stretch myself.

My first husband, Lee, was also one of my greatest teachers. I truly loved him, but the biggest benefit of marrying him was that he would stand up for me against my mother. Unfortunately, I ultimately needed to do this for myself and eventually learned to stand up to him instead of my mother, who had passed away.

CHAPTER 3

Coming Out of the Spiritual Closet

Like everyone who feels the need to become the Divinely Upgraded version of themselves, I felt compelled to learn everything I possibly could about combining my human experience with my Divine Soul Nature. I was also absolutely terrified about letting ANYONE else know what I was doing and studying. I tried desperately to be "normal" and not show the world who I was becoming.

I was not only in the spiritual closet, but I was also in the far back of the closet behind all the shoes and clothes and some boxes! I had to fight my way to the front of the spiritual closet to even begin to think about opening the closet door! Does that sound like anyone you know? Perhaps you?

I personally believe that we Light Workers (yes, YOU are one too) have experienced lifetimes where it was literally not physically safe to come out of the Spiritual Closet. Even as recently as the Salem witch trials, we were stoned to death, drowned or burned at the stake! Talk about an incentive to NOT let anyone know if you were "spiritually gifted!" Eek!

Our survival instincts, which are located in the most ancient part of our brains to ensure our survival as a species, will also kick in to keep us "safe." Unfortunately, they don't always understand that doing something different is not the same as being in danger of being killed and/or eaten by a bear! We all hate feeling as if we are different or don't fit in. I cannot express the amount of ridicule and derision I experienced at the hands of my second husband as I began to stretch my spiritual wings. I am so grateful that I had the courage to stick with it! I was actually shocked when I went to a writing class many years ago where the instructor (Tom Bird) had the audacity to talk about all things spiritual so casually. It was as if he were simply stating that the sky is blue or that the weather we have been having lately has been very nice! I can remember covertly looking around to see what everyone else's reaction was to such heresy! Shockingly, no one was the least bit concerned. And most of the people were nodding in agreement. I had been edging toward the door of the spiritual closet at that time. After that evening class, I took another step toward the door and put my hand on the doorknob.

Thank goodness I was able to find more like-minded people after that and began to explore trying to embody spiritual principles instead of just reading and dreaming about them.

The great news is that we are all safe to come out of the spiritual closet. The time to explore and try on your Spiritual Upgrades is now!

CHAPTER 4

We are Energy Beings and have a Spiritual Anatomy

Just as we each have a physical anatomy, we also have a spiritual anatomy! We have a series of spinning energy wheels called *chakras* that anchor our souls into our bodies and allow our soul to animate our amazing bodies. We are so very much more than "just" our physical bodies. It is a miracle that we can shoehorn a part of our vast souls into these bodies and experience the magnificent beings we all are. We were engineered to do just that.

There are seven major chakras in the body and many above our head as well. The lower-level chakras allow us to be grounded fully into our bodies and to the Earth plane. The higher-level chakras allow us to access our spiritual knowing and bring it into our human experience. The heart chakra is the transition chakra that also acts as an antenna to let us know whether what we are doing is in alignment with our soul or not. How do you know if your actions are in alignment with your soul? Ask yourself how you feel. Do you feel invigorated, or do you feel rather flatlined about a certain action? Or do you know that what you are doing actually hurts you in some way? When we feel absolutely giddy about what we are about to do or are doing, we are tapping into the energy of God or Source. We are bringing vital force energy into our bodies for us to create our lives! When we are out of alignment, however, we will actually have less energy to create our lives. It is almost like the battery on your cell phone. When you are plugged in to Source and who you really are, it is like having your phone plugged in to an infinite battery. When you are not plugged in, your battery can really drain itself quickly. When that happens, the only thing you have the energy to do after a day of work is to go home, have a bite to eat, drink a glass of wine, and veg out in front of the TV! Is that what you came here for? I don't think so! If it is, then this book is not for you. If you are ready to step up into your own Divinity and literally transform your life, then this IS the place for you.

Let's talk a bit more about our spiritual anatomy.

Spiritual Anatomy ...

We have an energy anatomy as well as a physical anatomy! As I said earlier, we are much more than these physical bodies. However, when we choose to incarnate, our souls need a way to anchor into and animate these fabulous bodies that allow us to learn and experience so much. The way the soul anchors into a physical body is through chakras (which means wheels of light in Sanskrit). Our bodies need more than food, water, oxygen, and love. They need an infusion of Divine Source Energy as much or more than food and water. This is how we receive the energy to run our bodies. Chakras are the conduits that keep our souls grounded into our bodies. They need to spin/vibrate cleanly to keep the body/soul connection clear and a good flow of energy going. Just as our physical bodies need food, water, and temperate conditions to survive, our souls that are housed in these bodies need Divine Energy to stay in these bodies.

Let's talk about the various chakras and how they function. Typically, you can't "see" your chakras, but you can certainly visualize them in your mind's eye. Remember when you were a child and played pretend or make believe? Do that again here. I want you to imagine the colors of the rainbow. These are the colors of your chakras: red, orange, yellow, green, blue, indigo, and violet. They correspond to particular areas of your body. They are also called your major chakras and are embodied (in your body). You have other primary chakras, but they are not located in your body.

Your Major Embodied Chakras

Chakra #1: Base Chakra. This chakra vibrates/spins to the color of a beautiful, vibrant ruby-red color. It is located at the base of your spine and allows you to be "grounded" into your body. It helps you meet your physical needs. This is the chakra that affects your connection to "tribe," society and family. Any time your 1st chakra is not functioning at its best, you will experience tiredness and feel as if you are not entirely present in your body. In addition, if your 1st Chakra is low, you may find you don't feel safe or loved or cared for or have a sense of belonging. It is particularly important for this incarnation that you allow yourself to have your physical needs taken care of. If you are not functioning as well as you would like in the physical world, it is probable that your 1st chakra needs tending to or recharging. The really cool thing about healing your energy body is that if you heal any tears or blockages before they actually manifest into the physical, you can stay healthy your whole life. So, what do you need to do to recharge and clear your 1st chakra? And all your other chakras? This will be covered under the chakra-clearing meditation at the end of the book in the appendix.

Chakra #2: Sacral Chakra. This chakra vibrates at a beautiful, clear, vibrant orange color. It should be the color of a perfectly ripe and luscious orange. This chakra is the center of your money and sexuality. It is located 2-4 inches below your navel. It feeds your primary sexual organs whether you are male or female. Your ability to have a healthy sex life and to feel like you have an abundance of money is determined by the health of your 2nd chakra. If the energy level of your 2nd chakra is low, you may feel a lack of interest in sex or not even feel sexy. You may also feel as if there is never enough money to go around – that you have more month at the end of your money! Recharging this chakra will help you improve both your money and sexuality.

Chakra #3: Solar Plexus. This chakra is a beautiful, lemon yellow and is the seat of personal power. It is located just above your navel and is at the solar plexus. It is also the center of your self-esteem and ability to set and move forward in your personal goals. Your sense of confidence and even charisma comes from a properly functioning, well-developed 3rd chakra. If your 3rd chakra is underdeveloped or even damaged, you will suffer from a lack of confidence or even a feeling of powerlessness or out of control-ness. You can also have an overdeveloped chakra that will cause an excessive sense of entitlement, super ego, or even narcissism. The best thing in all cases is balance. A perfectly balanced 3rd chakra should be a lovely, lemon-yellow color that is clear and unblemished. Also be sure to "look" for energy leaks which come from damaged or torn chakras. Remember that when you "look" at your chakras, you are seeing them in your mind's eye.

Chakra #4: Heart Chakra. This chakra governs your relationship with yourself and others. It is actually associated with 2 different colors. Officially it is green – the gorgeous emerald green that is clear, calm, and soothing. The heart chakra is also associated with pink – the color of love. Either visualization will work to clear your heart chakra. Green is the color of an enormously powerful healing light and is also the color associated with Archangel Raphael, who is the primary healing angel. The heart chakra is also the transition chakra between the lower chakras that ground us into our bodies and the upper chakras that are more of a spiritual connection. In fact, the new breed of Upgraded Spiritual Human Beings that we are ushering in right now are learning to integrate all the chakras better so there is not such a division between physical and spiritual. We are ascending to become beings who bring spirit into the physical more and more. We are literally creating heaven on earth. The main chakra that does this is the heart chakra. We are ushering in more and more love and light into our world. As Neo said in *The Matrix* — "Upgrades." We are upgrading our species. This is an extremely fascinating and fun time to be incarnated into the physical world! Enjoy the ride and be as excited as a child about whatever comes next. And know that it all gets put out into the world through our hearts!

Chakra #5: Throat Chakra. This chakra vibrates at a beautiful robin's-egg blue or aquamarine blue and is the center of communication and self-expression. This is where you speak your truth and communicate with others! This is either verbally or in written form or both. If you feel any tightness in your throat, you need to do a clearing or healing or recharging of your throat chakra. This is how you communicate with others, so it is critical to make sure it is healthy and functions properly.

Chakra #6: Third Eye Chakra. This chakra is located between and slightly above your physical eyes and vibrates a gorgeous color of indigo (deep blueish purple). This is the center of intuition, vision, and truth. It is the seat of your clairvoyance center. You may or may not see other-worldly things (such as angels) with your physical eyes, but this is where your mind's eye is. This is also the center of your imagination and creativity, which is especially critical when working on any spiritual endeavor.

Chakra #7: Crown Chakra. This chakra is located at the top of your head and vibrates a clear, cool violet. This is the gateway to the Divine All That Is. It is also the center of free will and choice. If you are feeling particularly stuck, ask yourself if you have been giving yourself enough freedom, choices, or options. Or have you been a stern taskmaster with yourself?

Major Chakras Outside Your Body...

Chakra #8: Soul Star Chakra. This chakra actually resides outside of your body, about a foot above the top of your head. This particular chakra resonates to the color silvery white and is the center of common sense and rational thought.

Chakras #9 - #12. These chakras are above the crown chakra and the 8th chakra and connect your body (physical and etheric) to your soul and allow "downloads" from your soul and Higher Self as your mind requests info.

You didn't know you had so much more to your anatomy, did you? We all know and accept other things we can't see with the naked eye, so this is just another one of those things! Take care of your energy body and it will keep you much healthier and happier! Try to emulate a child who channels divine life energy naturally, without any hesitations or judgments. In fact, shifting your energy just a tiny bit will bring massive results if you let it. I believe in you! Just go do it!

CHAPTER 5

Wear Your OWN Energy

Did you know that you may be wearing someone else's energy in addition to your own? One of the things we all do until we are made aware of it is that we end up taking on energy from other people. I am not talking about the energy swapping that occurs in our everyday lives. I am talking about when you literally take on someone else's sadness, anger, impatience, fear, etc. This is never a positive choice. If we want to create the best possible version of our life, then we need to be congruent with who we are. That certainly includes not wearing anyone else's energy or taking on anyone else's problems. In fact, there are lots of times we become corded in with the people in our lives, which can also be a problem, and an energy drain for you! Just remember (I know, I sound like a broken record) that you are a Divine Being. You have the ability to draw energy directly from Divine Source energy, which is limitless. I call it high-octane energy. This also means that all the people around you also have that same ability. They do not need to have a cup of you (or your energy) rather than going directly to Source for energy to power their lives. You are not responsible for them, either. It can feel wonderful to be so "needed," but it is not healthy for either party. Obviously, I am not talking about your small children, although one of the most empowering things you can do for your children is to view them as the Divine Beings they are. They need your help navigating the physical world safely until they can handle it themselves. Teach them to wear their own energy, too!

When I talk about wearing your own energy, I am also talking about how we will just pick up bits of fear, anger, un-deservingness, etc. All these negative thought forms will bring your vibrational level down.

So how do you determine if you are wearing your own energy or not? Use your imagination and creativity. Imagine yourself under a shower head that comes from directly above your head. Instead of water, it showers Divine White Light down onto your body and soul. This goes all the way to the center of Mother Earth to help you ground into your body completely. This lovely White Light will not only clear away energy that is not yours, but it will also align the polarity of your cells so that they are functioning in the most efficient way possible. When you complete this shower, your body will feel invigorated and refreshed. You will also feel quiet. This is how you know you were not wearing just your own energy. You go from feeling a bit unsettled or fearful or frenetic to feeling peaceful and calm.

Another way to clear your energy, especially if you feel like you are corded in with another person or people, is to call on Archangel Michael to lovingly cut the cording with them and gently cauterize it so that neither of you is leaking energy. Again, you will know if this works based upon how you feel in your body. My indicator is that my body and mind feel much calmer and quieter. Such a nice feeling. Just so you know, the other person may reach out to you since you are no longer giving them a cup of "you." They want their energy boost. Simply remind yourself that they are also a Divine Being and do NOT an energy boost from you. It can be easy to jump back into the drama of the situation that they might create to get their fix since you have most likely been corded in with them for a while. Just learn to step back and not engage. Don't beat yourself up if you do get sucked back in. That is probably going to happen. But then you can firmly step away again.

I know some of this sounds somewhat uncaring, but the most loving and caring thing you can do for your loved ones is to be clear about your own energetic boundaries and view them as the Divinely perfect beings that they are as well. Send them love but don't engage in the drama. That creates a discordant energy exchange you do not want.

One additional way to clear your energy so you are wearing just your own energy is to center yourself, call in your guides and angels and then smudge yourself with sage or sweet grass or whatever smudge stick you would like. Whatever feels appropriate. You are your own Spiritual Authority. So, trust your own feelings!

I realized recently that a friend's 4-year-old daughter had picked up some negative energies when we were in Mexico. I didn't want to scare her, so I created a game about it. I had her clap her hands together and rub them vigorously back and forth. Then I had her start at the top of her head and "wash" her whole body with her hands. When she was done, I had her raise her hands above her head to give any "cooties" to her angels. She giggled and did it. She had been extremely hyper for the whole trip until we did this. As soon as we were done, she laid down to rest and ended up taking a three-hour nap. She was a totally different person after this clearing. Obviously, the nap didn't hurt either, but she hadn't been able to calm down for a nap before the clearing.

You can do your own energy clearing and wear your own energy! All it takes is just a little shift in energy awareness and management.

CHAPTER 6

Introducing Spiritual Tools

Spiritual Tools are simply various techniques that help you connect with Spirit and the Voice of Your Soul in a way that is a bit easier to understand and hear. There are at least 25 different Spiritual Tools. We will be covering many of them throughout this book. In addition, I have written a workbook to be used with this book or to stand alone that discusses each tool and allows you to practice with each one. This allows you to find the tools that will become your "go-to" tools. One of my favorite tools is the pendulum.

The Care & Feeding of your Spiritual Tool – The Pendulum...

I am so fortunate that over the years I have developed a real connection with my pendulum as a spiritual tool. In most cases, it really is my go-to tool. The pendulum is a remarkably simple tool yet is incredibly powerful and helpful. I have looked for books over the years to help me use my pendulum more effectively and have not really found anything that really resonates with me the way I would expect it to. So, I have chosen to write my own section about pendulums.

The pendulum is simply some sort of weight or stone that can be suspended from a string or chain. The power of the pendulum is that it allows you to tap into your subconscious mind, your Higher Self, and your guides and angels. The good news is that you get to choose whom you wish to contact. Your pendulum does not have a mind of its own nor is it a sentient being. It is simply a reflection of the knowingness you already possess or your connection with your Guides and Angels.

How do you pick out your first pendulum? I suggest that seek a fairly simple design. The pendulums I have used in the past that were ornate were very pretty to look at, but they didn't work as well as the simple ones. My favorite pendulums at this point are simply a sphere of some sort of stone or crystal with a metal pointer, attached to a chain. There is no such thing as the wrong pendulum, but some work better for you than others. So, when you are looking for a pendulum, it is best to find one in person so you can use all your senses in determining which one you want. Once you have been attracted to a couple of pendulums, put them in your hand so you can feel how they feel to you. If this is the first time you have dealt with a pendulum, you may be feeling anxious about whether you can make it work. In fact, at first, I had this exact same problem. However, I have found a wonderful way to overcome that fear. As you know, we all have major chakras up and down our spine & out the top of our heads. We also have minor chakras that are in many parts of our bodies. The one I want you to utilize in learning to use your pendulum is your hand chakra. The palms of your hands have minor chakras that are always either receiving energy or sending energy.

Before you use the pendulum, place it in your non-dominant hand and cup the other hand over it. Call on Archangel Michael to clear this pendulum and attune it to your use. Don't worry if you don't end up keeping that pendulum. It will just dissipate to neutrality afterwards. Once you feel that the pendulum is attuned to you, you can try it out.

Hold the pendulum in your dominant hand by the bead that is at the top of the chain. Make sure that it is between the thumb and forefinger. Keep your other fingers relaxed, but away from the chain. You do not want your fingers pushing on the chain! Next, hold the pendulum above the palm of your non-dominant hand. The pendulum should not be touching the palm of your hand but should be about an inch above the palm. What you will see happen is the pendulum will start tracing the chakra in your hand. If your hand chakra is closed (which it may be), just visualize yourself sending energy out of your hand or allowing energy to come into your hand! That should get your pendulum moving! Once it does, you have a body of proof that you have found your pendulum and can indeed make it work. Yay!!!

When you get your pendulum home or to a place where you can be quiet and uninterrupted for a bit, go ahead and clear it before you start using it. There are several, easy ways to do this. One way is to call upon Archangel Michael to clear it while you send energy through your hands. A second way is to run the pendulum under water – even from a faucet is fine. The third way would be to smudge it with sage or sweet grass. In all three clearings, be sure to set your intention that the pendulum be cleared and attuned to your energy.

Once it is cleared you are ready to ask your pendulum some questions. Before you ask questions, you need to know that the pendulum is limited to "yes," "no," or "maybe" answers, so the quality of your questions is very important. Also, you need to see what a "yes" motion is for you and what a "no" motion is for you.

Get into a comfortable position. I like to be seated with my right elbow on my desk and my left hand over my heart. I do this to remind myself that I want to drop into my heart to get the most accurate, loving answers possible. Call in your Higher Self as well as your Guides and Angels. Remember, you have a staff of helpers who are on call and on demand for you at all times! Ask for the highest and best answers for the situation. Now, it's time to try it out.

Sit quietly and ask your pendulum to show you what a "yes" would be. Don't look at your pendulum for several seconds, because you may influence the results. Then look. For me (and everyone is different) a "yes" is a circular motion – either direction. Once you have gotten a clear response, then ask for what a "no" is. Again, note what that is. This should not change once you start using your pendulum. In fact, it should not change from pendulum to pendulum. Can you imagine how confusing it would be if each pendulum you owned had a different motion for "yes" or "no!" YOU are the common denominator. It really is what you decide it will be.

Now you may begin asking questions. However, since you have no confidence in your pendulum yet, do NOT ask any life-or-death questions. Start by asking simple questions like, "is my Granddaughter a girl?" Clearly something like that is obvious, but don't ask anything that is emotionally charged. At least not yet. Also, you are the boss!!! I don't know if I have emphasized that enough yet, but you are your own Spiritual Authority. If your pendulum starts getting wishy-washy, stop it and insist that it give you clear answers. Sometimes, the problem will be you! You must ask clear questions. Just like our computers, your angels and guides only answer the questions they have been asked. Not the questions you meant to ask. I have also found that our pendulums (and Spirit, Guides, Angels, and Subconscious minds) are quite literal, so make sure you are clear about the questions that you ask. I will give you a few samples at the end of this chapter.

What sorts of things might you wish to use your pendulum for? It is only limited by your imagination! Did you know that you can even talk to your own body to help you determine what is going on with it? You can ask about what is going on in relationships and in various life situations. I have even used my pendulum to connect with animals. I have asked dogs or cats who were clearly suffering if they were ready to leave their physical forms. And I get answers! We can tune in to so many things that the rational mind would tell you was impossible or ridiculous! Don't be afraid to try different things. In fact, I now do property clearings and blessings using my pendulum. I can get so much more information that way. You don't have to be psychic to know that things may not feel right in a house. Remember, we are all energetic Divine Beings. However, you can ask if there are earthbound souls in a house/property. You can also ask if there are any portalways or even gateways to other dimensions. And then once you know, you can clear these things, because YOU are a Divine Being. Believe in yourself and what you know deep in your soul! You can connect with your guides and angels anytime you want.

I spoke earlier about my own difficulties using a pendulum, so I would like to tell you my story. I was absolutely positive that this would be a tool I would love to use. However, I was a big fat failure about getting my pendulum to work! Fortunately, my sister was learning to use her pendulum about the same time as I was trying. She was having more success, so I asked her to show me. She stood against a desk or table and allowed her body to move slightly as well. She also held her left hand against her heart. I was shocked and thrilled! It finally worked. So don't be dismayed if it doesn't work for you initially. Just keep trying! In fact, another thing you might try is to start the pendulum moving gently and then ask it to show you a "yes" or a "no." Sometimes we need a little bit of momentum to get us going.

Quick side note: do not hold your pendulum over your palm when you are asking questions. The only reason you held the pendulum over your palm initially was so you could see that the pendulum can move without you moving it. However, you want real answers once you start asking the questions rather than just seeing what your hand chakra is doing.

Are your pendulums ever wrong? Of course, they are. There may be several factors to consider. For one thing, ask the most clear, concise questions you can. I also try to ask the same question in a different way, just in case I asked the first question in a way that was not clear. Also, if you are asking about other people, remember that they have free will and choice. Your pendulum can only answer based on this instant in time. The world is a fluid place, so things change all the time. The energy can change as a result.

If using a pendulum to connect with your own team of Guides and Angels sounds like the tool for you, I have created a 5 Module self-study course to help you learn to trust the answers you receive. Go to my website: www.EarthAngelTools.com to sign up.

Oracle Cards/ Angel Cards/ Tarot Cards...

One of the most amazing spiritual tools out there today are the Oracle/Angel Card Decks. These have evolved from the original Tarot Cards. There are many, many choices now, which is fabulous. You can choose from Angel or Archangel Cards, Fairy Cards, Dragons, Ascended Masters, Spirit Animals/Totems, Past Lives Cards, Akashic Record Cards, Updated & Simplified Tarot Cards, to name a few! To simplify the discussion about how to use them, I will refer to all of the oracle card decks as Oracle/Angel Cards. Oracle/Angel cards work through the Law of Attraction. You will attract the exact right cards that you need/want to see right now. Before you pooh-pooh this, let's go through what you do to give yourself a reading. And don't worry! You can easily do readings for yourself (and eventually others if you want). These can be amazingly helpful and accurate. Remember, you are an Intuitive, Divine Being.

The first thing you need to do is to purchase a deck of Oracle/Angel Cards. These are available online or even at bookstores like Barnes and Noble. Your very best bet is to go to your local metaphysical bookstore and find a deck that resonates with you. You will know the deck that is best for you when it seems to jump out at you in some way. Perhaps you are attracted to the color of the box or the artwork, or it may even seem as if there is a light shining on the deck. When you see/feel/hear that, then you know you have found your card deck! When you get them home, you need to take them out of the box, and they need to be attuned to your specific energy field. Remember that you are an Energy Being. Each of us has a different vibrational frequency, so you need to attune your deck to you. If ever you loan your deck out to someone, be sure to re-attune it to your own energy again before you use it.

One of the things I like to do before I even attune the cards is to look at every one of them. I love seeing the artwork and each message. It is important to really get a feel for the cards and their energy. Remember that when you do give yourself a reading, everything is a part of the reading. If your eye is drawn to the vase of water in the upper left-hand corner of the card, then that is part of the reading.

The way you attune the cards to you is you put the deck of cards in your non-dominant hand, with your palm up. Then place the dominant hand over the cards so they are between both hands. At that point, call in Archangel Michael (who is the bouncer and clearing/protection angel) and ask him to clear the cards and attune them to your energy. Hold that for a few moments until it feels like it is complete. You are then ready to do your own reading.

My favorite way to give myself a reading is to really shuffle the cards. Most angel cards and oracle cards and tarot cards are larger than playing cards, so they can be difficult to shuffle in the same way. Play around with them until you figure out the best way for you. I break them up into small chunks and keep putting them in the front and the back. No matter how you do it, you want to make sure you shuffle enough so you don't feel like you are just pulling consecutive cards.

The next thing you need to do is to set your intention for this reading. Your intention may simply be the question you want answered. You may ask the angels or oracles for guidance for the situation you are inquiring about. Just be clear. Frequently, my intention will be that I want a reading that is for my highest and best good. I find these readings very illuminating.

I usually choose to do a 3-card spread since three cards will give you a good snapshot of what you might want to be working on or give you the most detailed information. I spread the cards and pick what "feels" right to me. Remember, there is no right or wrong way to do this. It is amazing, though, that the exact right cards will come up. I can tell you there have been times where I have pulled cards that I have argued with! I have said, "No that does not make sense." Then, thinking I must not be clear or focused, I have then picked up the cards and reshuffled them so I could pull three more. I cannot tell you how many times I have pulled at least one of the original cards and the other two were basically the same message as the other two original cards. It can be a little freaky. At that point you then need to just really look at the cards to receive the message your angels are sending you. One quick reminder: You are the one who gets to interpret the reading. You are a Divine Being. Trust your own intuition. You are your own Spiritual Authority.

I would also recommend that you get a notebook to record your Angel Card readings for yourself. It can be very confidence-building and validating for you. You can read for yourself every single day if you want. The more you play with your cards, the better they will work for you because of your confidence level. Make sure you make this fun and playful. I have given angel cards to various friends throughout the years and my experience is that they made giving themselves a reading much too big of a deal, so they actually quit using the cards. Like the Nike commercial says, "Just Do It!"

I took my Archangel Oracle Card deck over to a friend's house one day soon after his mother-in-law had passed. Her passing had hit his wife and him quite hard and they were both still really grieving. I had never done an Angel Card reading for anyone else at that time, so I was a little terrified, but felt compelled to do it. So, I pulled out the cards and shuffled a little bit as I was praying over the cards. I asked our angels and guides to give us the most comforting reading possible. One card fell (leaped, actually) out of the deck as I was shuffling. It landed face up on the coffee table. The card was the "Hello from Heaven" card featuring Archangel Azrael. We both looked at the card, then each other and burst into tears. His much-loved Mother-In-Law was so clearly with us right then, letting us know she was fine, happy, and watching over both him and his wife. It was beautiful! That was the most perfect confirmation we could have gotten!

Spiritual Playmates and Support Groups (Your Soul Tribe) ...

As you move forward on your spiritual journey, it is critically important to find a group of like-minded people to work/play with. We all have felt like we are all alone on this spiritual journey. However, that is not the case. If you look, you will find a good group of like-minded people with whom you can interact. It is so refreshing to talk to someone who has belief systems similar to your own. You can be playful and enjoy talking to people instead of hiding who you are for fear of being ridiculed. I understand that ridicule is not fatal, but it can make you feel isolated and alienated as well as in a state of questioning your beliefs.

Look around and see if you can find spiritual playmates or your Soul Tribe. What fun to challenge each other to come out of the spiritual closet. And terrifying!!! There is such a sense of belonging and excitement when you do come out as your true authentic self, so it really is worth it.

Psychics – Going to them ....

My very first experience with a "real" psychic did not happen until I was in my early 30s. I was in a very unhappy marriage and "just happened" to hear about a famous psychic who was in town for a few days. Appointments were available, so I decided to book a session. Just to be clear, I heard this on the radio when I was in my car. I "normally" never listened to the car radio – just cassettes (yes, cassettes) or to nothing. However, I believe we all have these experiences where you just "happen" to hear exactly what you need to know at exactly the right time. Anyway, I booked an appointment because it sounded interesting. I didn't really know anything about having a reading but decided to take a leap of faith and try it. As I said, I was in an unhappy marriage and was even in counseling to help me cope with what was going on.

The sessions that were available were only 30 minutes long and I brought a list of questions. Well, I might as well have been walking in with a giant poster board with all the questions listed for her to read! She was amazing! As soon as I walked in, she said she could see that I was in a difficult relationship and that it would be for my highest and best good to leave it and get my son out of that dysfunctional situation as well. She let me know that even though any child comes in to experience the vibration and life experiences of each parent, he had come in specifically to be with me. She let me know (even though I already "knew") that we had been incarnated many times before and that this was a continuation of the love we shared for each other. I was also concerned that my husband would end his life rather than getting clean and sober for his son and learn to live a more functional life. She did not come out and say that he was still on that path, but she did let me know that his choice was just that – his choice. She also stated that I was not responsible for his choices and that I did not need to sacrifice myself for him anymore. There were several other things she talked about, but I do not remember them now. I do know that everything she told me was profound and accurate and all I could do was stare at her and cry. I tried to get in for another session, but she was completely booked for the rest of her stay in Albuquerque. Her name was Aileen, but I don't remember anything else.

It was several years before I went to another psychic. I was really going for a Reiki treatment rather than a psychic reading. The Reiki (a type of hands-on healing) was very nice and gentle and soothing. However, as she was doing the healing, she began channeling for me. She offered some incredible advice and the love that came through was so nurturing and healing that I was hooked. Instead of doing more Reiki treatments, I switched to channelings/readings. She was every bit as amazing as my first psychic experience. And, good news, she lived in Albuquerque! I began to go to her every month or so. I learned so much and would play the recordings she made of our sessions repeatedly in my car. Her name was Betsy Coffman, who goes by Betsy-Morgan now. She has been such an inspiration and teacher for me. In fact, I decided that I wanted to do what she did, and I took her channeling class.

Learning to Channel ...

It was an amazing experience; not anything like what I expected. I thought I would be able to "see" words on a page like reading a book when I would start channeling for someone else. That is not the case. Channeling is literally the verbal interpretation of energetic messages from either your guides, angels, or even departed loved ones. You certainly get an impression of what they are trying to communicate to you, but you are the one who must translate it.

When I learned to channel, the process was to meet three guides through a very loving, protected guided meditation and visualization. The very first thing you do is learn how to go into a deeply relaxed, grounded, centered, and loving state. This is a type of meditation – which is not weird or scary. Just a reminder that this is best done by experienced channels such as Betsy or my wonderful sister, Jana Lynne. They hold a sacred space for you and help you lift your vibrational level up to a level where you can experience your guides. The guides that you meet when you learn to channel will probably not be the guides you work with going forward.

The first guide to show up was my grandmother, Mama Kate. She was my dad's mom. She came forward and kissed me gently on my forehead. This was my third-eye chakra and I felt it open, which really surprised me. It was such a loving gesture, however, and so completely natural, that I immediately relaxed and allowed the opening. In the meditation, the guide was asked to give me some sort of symbol or item that would mean something to me. Mama Kate handed me a lovely little gold sewing machine figurine, which caused me to burst into tears. She sewed all her life and taught me to sew. It was such a sweet, loving confirmation that it really was her.

The second guide who showed up was my first golden retriever, named Buie. I was really happy to see Buie! She had died an early death at the age of eight-years-old and I still missed her. Then she dumped a tennis ball in my lap! Buie was one of those dogs who was totally obsessed with tennis balls, so it was another strong confirmation.

The third guide was not a departed loved one, but a guide who brought a red glow behind my closed eyelids. I got a sense of immense energy but did not get a name or a sense of what the guide "looked" like. I was really into crystals at this time and was given a beautiful amethyst crystal in the shape of a massage wand. I loved it and gratefully accepted it even though I felt a little intimidated by the amount of energy I was holding when I was channeling Red. As I was writing this down for this book, I decided to use my pendulum to finally identify Red. It turns out that Red was Archangel Rafael. This now makes sense since I have been so extremely interested in energetic healing for so long. Decades in fact. I just could not fathom then that I would be channeling an Archangel in my first channeling class.

The next thing that we did after we met our guides, was we learned to speak while in the channeled state. That was an interesting experience. Even though you know what you are saying and feel as though you are just making all this up, when I listened to the recording a few days later, I could tell that it really was not me speaking. Betsy had us practice moving in and out of the channeled state. The other channeling student and I then asked each other questions while the other one was in the channeled state. Talk about terrifying! I didn't know this guy and didn't really know what to say in response to his questions. Finally, I opened my mouth and said the things that popped into my head. I was absolutely 100% sure he would just say that I was an utter idiot, and nothing was remotely helpful. Instead, he looked a little bit shell-shocked and told me that what I had told him was extremely helpful and accurate. What an amazing experience that was. We did that a couple of times, back and forth. His answers to me were excellent as well. I was incredibly surprised at how well it worked.

Amazingly, you can strengthen your own spiritual connection at any time. That is what this book is all about. Using what spiritual tools work best for you.

I would strongly recommend that if you feel the urge to visit a psychic, you should try a few different people. Some people will just connect better with you and your guides than others, just as you connect more easily with some people than others. This does not mean that the psychic your friend suggested as being wonderful for him/her will be a good fit for you. Above all, remember to listen to your own intuition about all things spiritual. You are your own spiritual authority!

CHAPTER 7

Energetic Property Clearings. My Story

I have been doing house blessings and clearings for many years. I found that as a Realtor as well as someone who is energetically sensitive, it was just a "no-brainer" that many, if not all, of the houses I listed and/or sold needed an energetic clearing. We are all energy beings and as such we leave our energetic imprints wherever we live. This is somewhat like having a lingering cooking smell left in the house. It can be good, or it can be bad. I know everyone has had the experience of walking into a house after the owners have had a nasty fight with lots of hurt feelings and anger, instantly feeling the echo of the negativity. Even if the couple has a smile on each of their faces, there is a real feeling of discomfort remaining behind.

I began to really be sensitive to these energies when I was out showing houses to various buyers or previewing for the buyers before I showed them the house. There were many times where I would walk in and simply turn around and walk out – even when the house looked good and even smelled good. It just didn't feel good to me. I know that every single person out there is tuned in to that in varying degrees.

I have come to refer to the residual energy as energy dust bunnies. These dust bunnies can be anywhere from just stagnant energy all the way to hostile, angry, scared, or hurt energy. It is critically important to shift or clear any negative energies in your house. And this needs to be done fairly regularly. It is like needing to change out the water in your fish tank. Just as the fish need to have clean, fresh, filtered water in which to thrive, you need fresh, clear, clean energy to be your best spiritually attuned human being. Yes, you can certainly still function, but not as well.

I had no real idea about all of this until my first husband passed away. I knew I was energetically sensitive, but was busy raising my son, teaching, and doing all the frenetic things we all do in our lives. The circumstances of Lee's passing were not happy. He was a brilliant, but troubled man who chose to medicate his feelings of inadequacy and unlovability first by food and then drugs. He ultimately became addicted to cocaine and even began dealing drugs to support his habit. I knew that I had to get out of the marriage or go down with him. I finally worked up the courage to say I wanted a divorce. As is the case with many of us energetically sensitive people, I always saw the positive potential in him rather than accepting his current choices. So, I allowed myself to be talked into staying in the marriage. And then I went into counseling since clearly, I must be the one with a problem. My angels were watching over me and helping me because I really did need to go into counseling. It allowed me to create a wonderful support group for myself. I am eternally grateful to all my friends who supported me and told me I wasn't crazy. Lee was still using cocaine even though he said he was not. His behavior got more and more bizarre. After three or four months, I finally worked up the courage to once again say I was done and wanted a divorce. It was not pretty, but he did move out and we were working on the divorce terms. Things came to a head as they usually do when the enabler quits enabling. Lee was very troubled and unhappy even before the drugs took over his life. He ultimately took his own life after a failed drug overdose occurred.

I was on the phone with his sister when I felt him come back to the house in spirit form. He had apparently killed himself at the gun shop he owned. It was as if he had physically walked into the house! There was a tremendous amount of anger and darkness.

Since I was still the co-owner of the gun shop, I got a call from the alarm company as well as one of his employees that the alarm had not been set. They were checking to see if everything was okay. It was not. Police had been called. My employee met the police at the gun shop and found Lee's body.

The shock set in. Calls and arrangements had to be made. I didn't really have time to notice that Lee was still with me at my house. Things were busy and chaotic.

Once the funeral service was over and all the family and guests and well-wishers had gone back to their own lives, I found myself being jumpy, nervous, and constantly looking over my shoulder when I was in my house. On top of that, one of my recurring dreams was that Lee was reconstituting his body (he was cremated) and coming back to life! I admit that I felt like I was going a bit crazy! I finally mentioned it to one of my best friends and talked to her about how nuts that sounded to me, even though I was certainly open to this sort of thing. It just hadn't really happened to me in such an In-Your-Face type of way.

My friend Bev was Cherokee and was, in fact, the person who taught me how to meditate as well as helping me start to heal my co-dependent ways. We were both adult children of alcoholics. I will never forget her unconditional acceptance and belief in what I was telling her. I felt a whole lot less crazy. She simply told me we needed to do a house blessing and clearing. She said she would make the arrangements, and we would have a group of 8 or 10 friends come over to my house and we would gently, but firmly and lovingly, escort Lee out of the house and on to his next journey. She was clear that he was simply stuck since he had left his body so violently and quickly and with such anger.

Before we could get the house blessing done, Bev had me call in some Native American (Cherokee) Animal Spirit Guides for protection and clearing so I would be able to sleep better. I had never done this sort of thing before, but I am a great student, so I dutifully called in the guides she told me to call in. The main one I called in was Little Deer, who was gentle and loving and yet very protective. It was like calling in a Totem Animal, which I guess it really was. Little Deer and the others surrounded the house with their loving, protective energy and finally allowed me to sleep. The angry and fearful energy in the house calmed down a bit, but it was clear that a house blessing and clearing was still needed.

On the day of the house blessing, a group of loving, supportive friends of mine came over. As I look back on it now, I can see how "outside the box" this was, but everyone showed up with an open mind because they knew it was important. They were all truly Earth Angels that day.

Bev came early to do an initial smudging of the house. Back then (1984) there were not the nice smudge sticks of sage and/or sweet grass, so Bev used her cigarette to smudge with the smoke. She smudged the entire outside of the house and then the garage, where Lee's energy was the strongest. In fact, his presence was so palpable there that I couldn't even go in. Bev went in and had a heart-to-heart chat with Lee, explaining to him that by this time he could see for himself that he had been mistaken about his beliefs about me and that it was time to release that anger and move on to his next experience. (She relayed these details to me later).

We all sat in the living room and Bev led us into a meditative, loving state. Each of us called in a deceased relative or loved one to help us clear the house and to gently and lovingly assist Lee to the other side, where he would have a chance for deep soul healing. I called in my grandmother, Mama Kate. I also called in my mother. We all sat in quiet meditation and allowed our guides to help us shift the energy. I had a great deal of anger, regret, and even fear to clear, so I had what seemed like a very long chat with Lee in my head and heart. And this time, he actually listened. After really "telling him off," I got to the place where I realized that I had loved him very much and in fact, still loved him even though we were divorcing. As soon as I got to that place of love and forgiveness, the whole energy of the room and the house shifted. He let me know he loved me too, and that made all the difference. He stroked my cheek and then lifted up and out of the house. The house became so calm and quiet that it was almost unbelievable. If I hadn't been directly involved, I'm not sure I would have believed it.

We all spoke about what had transpired and everyone said they felt the energy shift. We all experienced the feeling of grace and love all around us. It was a profound experience for us all.

This case was a bit extreme, but ever since that time, I have been a very firm believer in clearing the energy and blessing houses.

CHAPTER 8

How to do a Property Clearing & Why

I am currently a Realtor as well as a Psychic, Light Worker, and Spiritual Counselor in this lifetime. As such, I am constantly in houses and/or with people all day long. Each time I walk into a house I feel the energy of the house and all its inhabitants. I am not unique; each of us does this already. I just happen to be a little more cognizant of it. Just as it is important to clean your house and stage it to present it in the best light possible, it is important to clear and cleanse the energy in the house. I have never fully embraced Feng Shui, although I know it works. I always felt there were just too many rules for me to follow. I prefer to open my energy and senses to allow me to try things on and decide which way feels better. More of an energetic-sensing Feng Shui, so to speak.

I have already spoken about why I got into the house clearing and blessing "business." It is so important to live in a house that is your safe place – your sacred space, your sanctuary. People from all walks of life can and do really respond to the energy in a house when they walk in. After all, our house is or should be our own sacred space, our retreat where we can kick off our shoes, let down our hair and really be who we are. So, if you are looking to buy a house, it is important to learn to drop into your heart, open your energy and truly feel any house that you are considering as a place to live. Many of the people I have worked with over the past 35 years do this instinctively. We all show up for a reason in each other's lives. There are no coincidences. The people who tend to be attracted to me are more heart-and-feeling based. My job now is to help each person be even more heart based. I have actually asked my clients to take a deep breath and get centered in the house. I ask them to then feel the house. Feel the soul of it. To feel the energy in the house. To feel the potential of the house and decide if it could become a true home or haven for them. There are many times that I can energetically feel whether a house is a good fit for my client. However, as a practitioner, I must allow for the free will of the client. Only the buyer can decide for sure what truly resonates with him/her. I can tell you that there have certainly been times where I just wanted to tell my clients to get over themselves and move past their fears. If I'm really good friends with my clients, I can tell them that this was, indeed, their house. I have usually had to wait for them to catch up to that fact. I am happy to say that no matter what their decision-making process is, they almost always eventually bought the house that worked best for them.

Clearing your house for selling or when you have bought...

Back to sensing energy in houses. When you are getting ready to sell, it is even more important to understand the energy signature of your house. Of course, all the energy work in the world will not overcome a messy, dirty, smelly, over-priced house. So, your job if you are getting ready to sell a house is to do the things in the third-dimensional world that need to be done. The house must be clean and fresh. We must make sure it is uncluttered and that it has good curb appeal. Clear away unnecessary items. Rent a storage unit for the things you want to keep, but that don't need to be in the house while you are showing it. Once you are satisfied you have "spiffed" it up as much as it needs to be, ask a friend or your Realtor or a professional home stager to come over for an objective viewing. Once everyone agrees that the house shows well, it's time for the energy work for the house. Remember, your energy signature is all over the house! You may not necessarily realize it, because it's your own energy. Rest assured, however, it's all over the house. In addition to your energy signature, there is a phenomenon called energetic "cording." You are energetically tied to your house, whether you realize it or not. When you choose to sell your house and/or move on to a new one, you need to learn how to gently and lovingly detach yourself from your house, or you will push away any potential buyers for your house until you do this. Your job when you are selling your house is to lovingly cut the cord with your house. Be sure to walk around both the inside and outside of the house and appreciate it and thank it for being your home. Then call upon your angels and guides to help you release the house with all the love and appreciation in your heart for it. Ask that the house now be free to attract the perfect buyer for it. State out loud (yes, out loud) that you appreciate and love it and that you are both free to move on. Ask your angels to surround both you and your house with Divine White Light. Imagine a shower of white light cleaning and clearing the energy of both you (and all the inhabitants) and the house. Do this until it feels like you are no longer attached to the house.

The next thing you should do is a smudging. Smudging is where you use some sort of sage or sweet grass to clear away stagnant energy. These are the Energy Dust Bunnies I wrote of earlier. It is a really good idea to open windows and really air out the house and allow the energy to move! If the energy feels particularly stagnant, enlist the aid of children. Have children come in and laugh and run and play in the house. Everyone will be able to feel the energy come alive and shift into happiness and love. Nothing is more appealing than walking into a house that has the feeling of love, laughter, and happiness. This is what you want to create when you are presenting your house to sell. It is finally time for us to recognize that we are much more than just physical beings. We are indeed all psychics! We just have to remember who we are and not run away from that.

Smudging allows you to focus on the energy signature you are wearing. Both you and your house. Once you have picked a smudge stick that seems to be right for you – yes, allow yourself to pick it out by using your inner knowingness – get a lighter and the smudge stick and go to the front door of your house. Call in your guides and angels to help you bless and release the house.

You have a whole staff of guides and angels, whether you realize it or not. It has been my experience that one of the very best angels for house blessings is Archangel Michael. He is the "bouncer" angel. He will escort out lower vibrational energies from the house. He has a magnificent sword of light that brings in divine light and will cut the ties and attachment you have with the house. He is always at your disposal and wants to be called upon.

Okay, you are at your front door, and you have called in Archangel Michael and all your guides and angels and helpers and departed loved ones (if you want). Now what? Light your smudge stick. This may be one of the most difficult parts of the whole house blessing/clearing! Once it has burned a bit, blow out the flame and allow it to smoke. Typically, it is white smoke. As you stand at the front door of the house, close your eyes, ask the guides and angels to come to you now to bless the house and cleanse it. Move the smudge stick in a clockwise direction three times. You are moving the fresh, Angelic energy into the house. Once that is done, walk through the door and really open your energy so that you truly feel the house. This is no longer the house in which you raised your children or where you might have suffered loss or disappointment. It is a house that is now preparing its energy for a new owner or family. You are releasing it to allow that very thing to happen. Feel yourself working to love and appreciate not only the house, but also the people and/or pet who are attracted to it. Really move into your heart. As you stand inside the front door, ask Archangel Michael to help guide you as you walk through the first room. Your smudge stick should be smoking, and you walk around the perimeter of each room allowing the smoke to permeate all the edges and corners of each room. As you do so, ask that all the stagnant or sad or angry or hurt energy residuals be swept away and that the angels transmute these energies to love and light. Sometimes it will feel necessary to go around the room more than once. How do you know? Go with your feelings. If you don't know, just ask yourself, *if I did know, what would I do?* Follow your gut/hunch/intuition. Go through the whole house, clearing and cleansing and lightening up the house, room by room. I personally prefer to go from the bottom up if it is a house with more than one level. The most important thing, however, is to follow your own instincts. After you have smudged the inside of the house and it feels calm and quiet (yes, quiet is also a feeling), then thank the angels and move to the outside. You will want to do the whole perimeter of the house within reason and the yard – along the walls, too. Again, ask for the protection of the angels and for their help clearing away lower and/or stuck energies. Once that feels complete, allow yourself to really feel your house again and feel how wonderful it is now that the energy has shifted. You have done great work and your house will tell you how much it appreciates you. You will then want to call in protection for the house so that only love and light be allowed into it. If you wish, sprinkle some kosher salt along the exterior of the house so that the blessing is all along the outside.

Does this work? Absolutely. It is probably even more important that you, the homeowner, do the house blessing in conjunction with the letting go ceremony. I cannot remember how many times I have had perfectly wonderful houses sit on the market much longer than they should have because the sellers were holding onto the house so tightly that the potential buyers could not even see the house as a home for them. I would finally have a serious discussion with my sellers about really, truly letting go of the house. I found it was much like sprinkling fairy dust on the house once they do that! Magic happens when the energy shifts. What a joy and blessing it is to see that happen. Once the seller truly releases the house, they are then willing to make sure the price is right, the presentation is good, and their energy is not a blanket being held over the house.

There may be houses that need professional help for energy clearing. Sometimes the homeowner is too sad or heavy (energetically) to really shift the energy. There are also times when the people in the house have actually allowed darkness or dark entities to live in the house.

I have learned even more about clearing houses. Did you know there can be earthbound souls attached to the property? There can also be portalways or gateways where souls can come and go from different dimensions. Sometimes the property might have been designated as a sacred place or a battleground or even a burial ground! Obviously, I am not suggesting situations like the movie *Poltergeist*, but it can be very unsettling for you, especially if you are energetically sensitive (which is ALL of us!). This type of professional clearing is beyond the scope of this book, but just know that I am now able to do those clearings and move the earthbound souls along to their next experience. There are other people as well who can do this work if you feel that something more is amiss than just the Energy Dust Bunnies or shifting stagnant energy.

Whenever I represent a buyer in the purchase of a new home, I now do a clearing and attunement on their new house. Obviously, they would not have purchased the house if it did not resonate with them, but one of the things I do is to clear away the previous owner's energy and attune the house/property to the buyer's energy. It really makes a huge difference.

Vacation Property Clearings...

My wonderful husband and I went to France a couple of years ago to go to the French Open. We are both big tennis fans and players, so we wanted to go. Matthew surprised me with a wonderful château in which to stay for several days while we explored the French countryside. Of course, it was between 500 and 600 years old. It had been updated with bathrooms and electricity, but still was very old. When we got there, we were both exhausted from all the travel and related stress (such as driving down one-lane roads that were meant for two cars!). We went out for a lovely dinner and came back to the chateau and crashed. I never even thought of clearing the room. Well, at 2:00 in the morning I was jolted awake, just like a little kid who knows there is a monster under the bed. I found I had the covers pulled up over my nose and I was really freaked out. As I said, I do know how to clear this from any room/hotel/apartment I am staying in – I just forgot! So, I called in Archangel Michael and asked that the room be cleared for the duration of our stay. The room felt better, but not great. However, it was good enough for me to go back to sleep and get the rest I needed. We were gone much of the next day, but the owner of the chateau had a chef come in and prepare a fabulous four- or five-course dinner for us that evening. We dined with other guests who were also staying there and had a delightful time. We went to bed, and I was again awakened by the earthbound souls (aka ghosts) at around 2 a.m.! I was really grumpy about that, so I really stepped into my own spiritual authority and power. I again called on Archangel Michael, but also called upon other angels and just blasted those ghosts out of the room. In fact, I sent them out of the chateau! That made such a difference. I slept deeply for the rest of the night. In fact, I was the last one down to breakfast. I was pleasantly surprised that one of the cats who had been very aloof suddenly took a great interest in me at the breakfast table. The owner sat with us and talked about all the things that had gone wrong in the chateau when he closed it up for the winter. Finally, I mentioned that he had earthbound souls in the house that were disruptive to the level of poltergeists. The other guests were very interested as was he (or so it seemed). I had actually gotten a head count and there had been seven earthbound souls in our room. I explained the situation to him and offered to do a clearing if he wanted. Unfortunately, he never contacted me, so I guess he wanted the notoriety attached to having ghosts. And what self-respecting chateau would not have ghosts? Anyway, this was our last day, so after breakfast I went upstairs to pack the rest of my things. The cat who had been so aloof followed me all the way up to our room (fifth floor) and inspected every square inch of the room, including a large armoire that had felt creepy to me when we got there a couple of days before. The cat was a hoot. He/she even crawled into my open suitcase and stayed there until

I said he/she had to get out. I did explain to the cat that this was only temporary since I did not own the chateau. I did not have the authority to permanently clear the property. The cat rubbed my legs in a final thank you and left. Even Matthew remarked about the cat. Crazy times.

One of the things I learned from that experience is to clear any room or house I am staying in, even if it feels okay when I get there. So many times, I am tired or not tuned in when I arrive, but almost every place needs clearing.

Matthew comes from a large extended family, and we all get together every two years for a family reunion. One of the most recent ones was held at a hotel on the plaza in Las Vegas, NM. The hotel is renowned for its ghost population. I finally agreed to go to the reunion since I knew I could at least clear our room. Our room did indeed need clearing, so I cleared it. The next morning several people were complaining about not getting good sleep the previous night. I offered to clear the rooms (temporarily) for anyone who wanted me to. I ended up clearing eight or ten rooms for various people. One couple had brought their dog who had gone ballistic the day before. After the clearing, she was fine being in the room.

Just be aware that there can be many energetic impediments to the quiet enjoyment of your property. Trust your own intuition.

CHAPTER 9

Energetic Protection

It is amazing how many spiritually oriented books and online courses are dedicated to protecting yourself from psychic attacks, someone stealing your energy, or energy vampires. I must say that I used to buy into this myself. The really amazing thing is that energetically, nobody can do anything "to" you without your permission. Again, it bears repeating that you are a Divine Being and Your Will must be done! Now if you feel like you deserve to be punished in some way or if you feel like you have to give away some energy to help those around you, that's on you! No one is "stealing" your energy or placing a negative intention (also called a curse) on you without your cooperation. Be sure to remind yourself of that when you start using verbiage like "You MADE me do this!" or "This is all your fault!" You are NO LONGER a victim unless you CHOOSE to be! Don't forget this. Pay attention to the words you use when you talk about the things in your life. Remember that the same is true for your own self-talk. We have certainly all created habits over our lifetime that allow us the luxury of not having to think through every situation. A kind of knee-jerk, automatic reaction. We all do this so that we can free up energy and have time to do new things that interest us. Can you imagine how difficult it would be to have to think your way through every single thing that happens in your life?

I play tennis. The thing you must learn in tennis is to create muscle memory. This is why you practice. When you are actually playing, you cannot "think" your way through each shot. It is simply not possible. Every time my serve goes "off," I find myself tutoring myself about how to serve! Take it from me – it does NOT work! I have to go back to remembering what it feels like when I am serving well.

If you have created the "muscle memory" that there are energy vampires out there and that you have to watch out for them and guard your energy at all times, then you would be greatly served by doing a "pattern interrupt" on that thought pattern. The pattern interrupt is to remind yourself that you are a Divine Being! No one can "steal" your energy without your permission. You are safe!

When I say you are safe, I mean energetically. There is a saying that you shouldn't drive faster than your angels can fly. Just a reminder that our bodies are magnificent and amazing healers, but it's best not to put yourself into physically dangerous situations.

CHAPTER 10

What Does It Mean to be an Earth Angel?

Our Angels and Guides are constantly supporting and loving us at all times. They cannot intervene without our specific request unless it is a matter of life and death. So, it is important that you remember to ask for help and then be willing to hear and accept that help. In our everyday life, it is often difficult to hear/feel the subtle energies of our Angels and Guides. So what they do is gently, lovingly work through the people around us. I have found that I may be struggling with a decision or need some sort of clarification and will ask my angels for help. Sometimes, within moments, I will run into someone or receive a phone call or text that is the exact message I needed to hear.

Several years ago, I was in a very dark, hopeless place. My second husband was very ill with multiple medical issues, feeling suicidal and being an angry bully to me. Even though I knew none of his issues were my fault or responsibility, he did his best to blame me. No matter how hard I tried to lift myself up, I could not seem to do it. Finally, one day I was driving to my office and asked God and my Angels to help me RIGHT NOW! I did not ask very lovingly! I was terribly upset and felt totally abandoned. I walked into my office, checked my mail, walked back around to the front desk and "accidently" heard a tall, blonde woman ask for my broker, Tony. This happened all the time, so I did not think anything of it initially. However, I then did a double take. This woman was someone who was a nutritionist and spiritual healer whom I hadn't seen in several years. I turned around and called her name. It was indeed her! She said she had been driving by and got an irresistible urge to stop by the office to see Tony. Well, Tony was not just out of the office, but even out of the country at the time, she was clearly there as the answer to my prayer. She helped me immensely and to this day I am so very grateful to her for being aware and willing to listen to her own guides and angels. She was certainly my Earth Angel that day!

Spiritual Guidance comes to us from all sorts of different avenues. If you are not profoundly clairvoyant, clairaudient or claircognizant, your guides and angels must work through other people to help you get the information or message you are seeking in prayer. And it is truly amazing how often that when you are seeking guidance you will "just happen" to find the perfect answer in a book, or online, or even snippets of an overheard conversation from the people sitting next to you in a coffee shop!

It is your personal responsibility to listen to your own guidance system – your angels, guides, your body. You never know when you will be called upon to be someone else's Earth Angel. Always say what you feel nudged to say but be sure to filter it through your heart. If you say what you are being urged to say with love, you are indeed being enlisted into being an Earth Angel for your friend/client/acquaintance.

There may be times that you will find yourself urged to say things to people who you don't know very well or even at all. You need to be the judge of whether to say something or not, but you certainly don't want to be intrusive. I always used to say to go ahead and speak up when you felt divinely guided to say something to someone. However, I am modifying that at this time. We all have the choice to be fully present in our bodies and not "out there" being psychically nosey. We need to act with integrity about intruding on someone else's energy. Yes, we are all broadcasting our energetic frequency, which includes a lot of information. If you feel like it is really important to tell someone a message you are getting, please do so respectfully. You might even say something like, "I am getting a message from your angels or guides. Would it be appropriate for me to share with you?" Nothing is worse than someone coming up to you saying they have a message for you when you are not really looking for a message. Just employ the Golden Rule.

CHAPTER 11
What is Soul Shifting?

Did you know that your soul may not be the only soul in your body? In my practice as a Soul Realignment Practitioner and Intuitive Consultant, I have found this to be a debilitating situation for those for whom I have done readings.

There are many situations where you may be frustrated about why you cannot seem to do the things you want to in life and create the results you would like. I have found that many times this is because you are doing something called "soul shifting." This is usually a situation that has its roots in a past-life traumatic experience. Even though you have full consciousness of what actions you are taking, there may have been times in your life where you look back and ask yourself, *What the hell was I thinking when I did that?* What has most likely happened is that you have had other souls literally attached to your soul for several lifetimes and you are now letting them take control of your choices or actions some of the time so they can experience life. I liken this to allowing the "kids" to drive your car (your body). This means exactly what it sounds like. Your kids are taking your car out for a joy ride since they don't have and can't get a car of their own while their souls are attached to yours. Many times, I have found clients who are literally only in their own body for about 30% of the time! It is extremely difficult to create the life you want when you are in control only 30% of the time. Obviously, this is not a good situation for anyone — neither your own soul nor the souls that are attached to you. Once we have cleared this situation and sent the attaching/shifting souls on to their next experience, you will find that both your body and consciousness are noticeably quieter, calmer, and more congruent. You don't feel like you are being pulled in different directions by the kids who want to drive the car!

I had one client who was self-aware enough to realize that once we cleared the attaching souls with which she was soul shifting, she figured out that one of the other souls had clearly been the organizing soul who always helped her move. She told me she would go into a room to pack up boxes and just stand there – almost not knowing what to do! She actually had to tell herself that she could figure out how to pack the boxes efficiently and quickly by herself. I absolutely loved that she could tell me this.

If you are having difficulty moving ahead in your life, you may want to find out if you are soul shifting.

CHAPTER 12

Past Lives and Past-Life Regressions

I believe in reincarnation and have found what I consider proof that I have had many lives. I absolutely believe that our present life situations and characteristics are a result of not only our present life choices, but also our past-life choices. I mentioned earlier in the book that I was very keen on finding out who I had been in past lives. And I was not able to access that information. I was hoping I would just spontaneously remember my past lives and know everything and everyone I had ever been. Well, I was truly being protected by my angels. This sort of thing is not always healthy to know. The only lifetime in which you can make any changes is the present one that you are living. Obviously, there are some things that you carry over from lifetime to lifetime. The main reason for delving into past lives is to find the root cause of disempowering situations that you are once again creating! Past lives are interesting to delve into even so.

My very first official past-life recollection or experience happened when I was in my mid-twenties. My husband, son and father-in-law went on a short vacation trip up to Durango, Colorado. We took in the sights there and decided that we would go to Mesa Verde Park the next day. None of us really knew anything about Mesa Verde and were surprised at how far it was from Durango. I had no idea that I was about to have my first past-life recollection. We visited several of the Mesa Verde sites before we got to Cliff Palace. When I stepped off the ladder and turned around to look at the sights in Cliff Palace, I had an almost dizzying sense of deja vu. I absolutely knew I had been there before! As we took the tour, I kept seeing things and people flip between present life and past life. I was seeing the Anasazi! And I was one of them! In fact, I was really annoyed that I was required to stay on the tourist path. I "knew" where I needed or wanted to go, but I was not allowed. On top of that, I just knew what things were in the organization of the city. I even knew where we had put the trash! I knew where the group meetings were held and where I had lived! It was so exciting that my teeth were chattering. On the other hand, my rational mind was telling me that I just had an incredible imagination and to let it go. Just as most of us do, I listened to my mind and ego initially. Over the next few days, I journaled my experience and realized that it had been a true past-life recollection. I never doubted myself in that aspect again.

Brian Weiss has several books about doing past-life regressions so you can see who you were and what lessons you are bringing forward into this lifetime. I found this very helpful in a number of ways. The first few past-life regressions that I did were really great lifetimes, and I was very excited. I wanted to do more. One thing that I did keep in mind, however, is that this lifetime is the only one where I can make changes. The past lives might be helpful in explaining why I kept repeating certain patterns, but I could only view them like a movie. I could even feel the feelings, but I could not make any changes. Even with that attitude, I got a little hooked on doing past-life regressions for myself. I was willing to spend more time in the past and mulling that over rather than in making my present life better. I was doing spiritual escapism. Until I did a past-life regression where I saw myself calmly and matter-of-factly order the death of a deformed infant. I understood "my" attitude from the past, but I was so horrified as the present-day me, that I realized it was time to stop playing around with the past so much and to concentrate on the present.

In my present intuitive readings through the Soul Realignment modality, I have learned to do past-life readings for myself and for my clients that are much more matter of fact and much less emotionally attaching. We have all done things in past lives where we have injured or killed other people. Usually these are the people who have shown up in this lifetime as well. It is actually immensely helpful to find out what blocks and restrictions are alive and well in your energy body at this time, based upon past lives. The cool thing is that you can see how these things affect you without having to play them out completely with all the horror of seeing a rape or one of your loved ones being killed. I would highly recommend Soul Realignment for any and all spiritual seekers. A Soul Realignment Reading gives you tools to change the disempowering behaviors that are carried over from previous lifetimes. It is also incredibly powerful to be able to see where these behaviors came from and the soul story behind them. This is a quicker way to begin to shift and clear karma that needs to be cleared rather than taking many more lifetimes to clear the karma. Do it now in a deeply empowering way.

CHAPTER 13

Messages from Heaven

We all want to get a message of some sort from loved ones who have passed — or from our angels and guides. There are many ways our departed loved ones as well as our staff of spiritual helpers can contact us. One of the most common ways this happens is that you may start seeing feathers or coins or recurring/repeating numbers. The more you notice and acknowledge this, the more you see or experience them. Here are a few examples from my life.

My father was my first love. He was not perfect, but he was indeed perfect for me. Fortunately for me, he lived a fairly long life. He passed away at the age of 86. I have put in my order to pass away the way he did – he was living independently in his own house and completely taking care of himself. He had a morning ritual of reading the paper, working on the crossword puzzle and drinking his coffee. He was doing exactly that when he slumped over and left his body. As happy as I was that this was an easy and loving passing, I was devastated. Yes, I know his soul is still with us and that I can access him at any time, but when he passed, I just shut down. Then several things happened that reminded me that he could still communicate with me. The first communication happened was when I was staying at my dad's house right after he passed. I had a visitation in the form of a lucid dream. I saw him in a train, leaning out of the window, giving me his cute mischievous look, and blowing me a kiss. I woke up knowing that I had truly seen him and that he had gone through a fair amount of effort to give me that sign. The next time I knew he was with me, I was in a silly curio shop in Albuquerque's Old Town. There was a display of keychains that had different names on them that would light up with the sunlight. Most of the display was dark, but then one that had the name George on it started flashing. My dad's name was George. I could have overlooked it, but I realized it really was a message from my dad. After that I kept seeing license plates on the cars in front of me that reminded me of him. The most staggering one was "GEO444." I could not believe that one. 444 is the repeating number to let you know that your angels are with you and are standing by for any of your requests.

My second husband passed away by his own hand after enduring incredible pain and many debilitating illnesses. I was his support for that time period, so it was sad but also a great relief when he passed. He definitely wanted me to know that he was okay, but I also had had enough, so I was not listening. Eventually he got word to me through a psychic friend of mine that he was okay, no longer in pain, and that I had been right about the spiritual things I had been talking about for years. A side note here: I owe him a deep debt of gratitude for showing up in my life even though there was great difficulty. He pushed me to clarify my thinking and decide that I would ultimately write books and speak about spirituality. One specific thing that happened after he passed was rather remarkable. I was terribly upset about a situation that was developing in my life. I stopped in a Walgreen's store to pick up something. Three things happened almost simultaneously to tell me he was there supporting me. The first thing was that the song I played at his memorial service started playing through the store speakers. At the same time, I stopped and was right in front of the diabetes info area (Jim was diabetic) and then I literally felt a big hug from him. I broke down and started crying in the store, but I also felt oddly comforted.

All of us have departed loved ones who we wish we could hear from or talk with just one more time. Well, you can! You just need to pay attention and suspend your disbelief a bit. Your loved ones will probably not apparate at the foot of your bed, but they can let you know they are around you when you call on them. Pay special attention if you keep seeing feathers, repeating numbers, hearing a familiar favorite song or seeing their initials on the license plate of the car in front of you. If you allow yourself to be open-minded and allow for the possibility (I know, woo woo) that they can reach out, you really will start seeing signs everywhere. Be sure to journal your sightings because your rational mind will talk you into believing you are just making it all up! Give yourself the gift of creating a body of proof for yourself.

CHAPTER 14
Stepping into my Own Spiritual Authority

I spoke earlier about my religious and spiritual experiences and evolution. Now I will dive in a little deeper and more personally about how I have learned to step into my own spiritual authority in the hopes that it may resonate with your own journey.

As I said earlier, my first break with traditional religion was when I learned/heard about reincarnation. That resonated so strongly within me that I could not ignore it. I also could not continue going to my church on a regular basis as a result. I still loved many aspects of church life, but just did not feel quite as congruent as I wanted. One of the other breaks was that I had felt there were so many times we were treated like children. That we needed to be good little parishioners or spiritual beings and we would be rewarded when we died. If terrible things happened to us, it was considered the will of God, rather than anything to do with us or our choices.

This victimhood or powerlessness does not serve us as a species and certainly not me! And believe me, I have played victim and helpless many times in my life! The first person to call me on it was a massage therapist! I had broken my ankle several years before in a motorcycle accident. I was going to her to help me get more flexibility back and to strengthen it. So, as I was lying there on her table, she asked me how I created this injury. I just looked at her with my mouth open! I then mumbled something about it just being an unfortunate accident. She said that I could keep looking at it that way if I wanted, but that I had been part of the creation of the truck hitting my motorcycle. That I had in some way manifested the situation. Understand that the truck turned right into me — I had the right of way. Obviously, I had to really process this a bit. And she really helped me shift out of victim energy and take full responsibility for my life – the good, the bad, the ugly! It took me a few years to really shift out of the blame game, but you cannot say you are a Divine Being who is creating your own experience and still tell someone, "You did this to me!" These are not in alignment with each other.

One of the other breaks with religion came as I finally decided I did not need to turn myself into a pretzel to be a good little spiritual being. Obviously, being a good/kind/loving person is important, but this is for all parts and times of your life. I cannot tell you how energetically yucky it is to see someone act so pious and spiritual on Sunday morning, but then stab you in the back on Monday in the guise of "it's just business." I believe that if you are not energetically congruent in all aspects of your life, you are not living your best life.

One of the most difficult things I have had to learn to embody is that I am deserving of a fabulous life no matter what "bad" things I have done in my life before now. I know that our actions (choices) always carry consequences and create karma for us. The main guideline is that every single one of us is a Divine Being who came here to the Earth Plane to experience ourselves in a place where we clearly see the consequences of our actions. Suffering is a choice! It does not always seem like that, but it is. The amazing aspect of our lives here is that we have free will and choice to create our lives. We can back ourselves into some really bad corners based upon this – and then yell at God for putting us there! God just allows us to create our lives using our own free will and choice. So, back to personal responsibility! The only rule about that is that we do not have the right to impinge on someone else's free will and choice. Doing that does indeed create karma that will affect you. It may not in this lifetime, but certainly will eventually.

What do I mean by Stepping into My Own Spiritual Authority? I mean that I have finally really understood that I do not answer to any outside spiritual authority figure. I have my own direct connection with God or Source, and I determine what is right for me based upon my own inner knowingness. I no longer give my power away to other people or to an outside spiritual authority.

One of the things I have had to really work on is a deep, soul-level feeling of deservingness. That I deserve to have a satisfying, wonderful life. And knowing that it is literally my birthright. It is yours, too!

Our lives were originally designed to be easy, joyful, loving and fulfilling. What happened? We forgot how to use Divine Law. We forgot to create our lives using our Divine Soul Blueprint. We forgot to use our soul level gifts. How do we determine what our gifts are and how to use them? I know I have said it before, but I highly recommend a Soul Realignment Reading! If not from me, then from someone who does this work. It is such a transformational reading. Do NOT go into a reading unless you are serious about shifting your life. If you approach it intellectually with an "isn't this interesting" attitude, do not bother to do it. Doing a Soul Realignment Session can help you significantly transform your life. Do it as a gift to yourself to really give yourself a boost up in your own spiritual development journey. When you are ready, it is an amazing catalyst to allow you to transform your life. Learn to BE your own Spiritual Authority!

CHAPTER 15
What are the Akashic Records?

You are a Divine Being who has had many lifetimes. You are the sum total of all your lifetimes as well as all your current life experiences. The Akashic Records are your energetic permanent record or database of all the choices you made in each lifetime. We all create karma as we go merrily through our lives. That karma is with other people in our lives. Obviously, if we create negative karma, then that must eventually be cleared or else you are stuck repeating the circumstances that energetically match that karmic situation. In other words, if you killed someone in a previous life, you recreate that karma in your life or lives until you have cleared or balanced that karma. We will all eventually clear all our energetic karma, but wouldn't it be a remarkable thing if we could clear the karma mindfully and "on purpose" instead of haphazardly through lifetime after lifetime? Good news! You can!

Akashic Records are a perfect place to start if you are trying to figure out why you keep repeating certain disempowering situations in your life. There's an old saying about moving to a new place to change your life. The only problem with that is that wherever you go, you take you with you. All your baggage comes with you unless you make the conscious effort to clear that baggage. Many times, however, you may not even know where that baggage came from. There is tremendous power when you know the underlying root cause of the situation you are trying clear. Clearing your old disempowering beliefs and karma will allow you to pull those weeds out by the roots instead of chopping them off at ground level and watching them grow back. There are many different ways to access your Akashic Records. This is deeply transformational work, so I highly recommend that you consult someone who does this sort of work rather than trying to figure it out yourself. I recommend strongly that you invest in your own spiritual transformation by having a Soul Realignment Reading and Clearing. It is a tremendously powerful tool for you to use to accelerate your own growth and ascension.

Just know that this is a tremendously powerful tool.

Past Life Regressions and Situational Readings...

Sometimes there are issues in your life that are much bigger than what has actually happened in this lifetime. I have found amazing clarity and healing by doing past-life regressions. Clearly, you should have some sort of belief in past lives before you choose to do this, especially if you are doing a self-guided regression from a recording. I have resonated with the concept of reincarnation since I was first introduced to it in my late teens/early 20's. I was raised Presbyterian, which I loved and enjoyed, but which felt incomplete to me. When I read *The Search for the Girl with the Blue Eyes*, written by Jess Stearns, which covered the topic of reincarnation, I just knew immediately that I had found the missing piece of the spiritual puzzle I had been looking for! This was truly a life-changing experience for me; I knew deep in my soul that I had lived many times before. I did not know how to find out what my past lives were, however. It is important to know that things in your life will and do unfold at the exact right time. You will not learn the lesson or hear the message until you are ready.

A quick caveat about delving into your past lives: THIS lifetime you are experiencing right now is the most important lifetime for you to be present in. Be here, now. If you really have an issue with someone or something in your life, it may be beneficial to do a past-life regression. Brian Weiss is the author of *Many Masters, Many Lives.* He has a wonderful relaxation and regression exercise that you can record and play back to yourself. If you are not experienced in guided meditation, you may simply wish to practice the meditation a few times. It is important to learn how to get your body to be quiet enough to listen to and hear the voice of your soul. This is also your Higher Self.

If you do not feel comfortable doing a past-life regression but can feel the importance of learning about past lives, I have a few suggestions. Start by writing down the sorts of things you are attracted to. For example, I have always been fascinated by pens, especially fountain pens and calligraphy pens. I always figured that I had some sort of lifetime that involved pens, but I never really knew why. One day a few years ago I had a clear picture of me as a small, Chinese man who did calligraphy and always had ink on his/my hands. It was so clear and real that I have absolutely no doubt it was a past lifetime.

In addition to seeing what things you have always been drawn to, start looking at your hands. You may realize you are seeing "your" hands, but they are not the hands currently attached to your physical body in this lifetime. The same thing goes with your footwear.

You may also simply spontaneously remember a past life when you visit a place for the "first" time. I know I mentioned it earlier, but one of my very first past-life memories was at Cliff Palace in Mesa Verde National Park. I was with my son, first husband, and father-in-law on a short trip to Durango, Colorado. On the way up, we stopped at Aztec and went through those Anasazi ruins, which were interesting. The next day, we went to Mesa Verde. We visited several of the smaller, more easily accessible sites first. Interesting, but no big deal. But when I climbed down the ladder to access

Cliff Palace, I had the strongest sense of deja vu! As I walked along the path open to the public, I kept seeing things switch from the current view with all the tourists and tour guides to an ancient view complete with a teeming, busy Anasazi village. Frankly, I was quite annoyed that I was not able to access some of the areas I felt I should be able to access. I "knew" things about how the village operated. Overall, it was a surreal experience. I later did a little research into the specific organization and daily operations of Cliff Palace and found out I was "dead on" in my impressions. Several years later, I did a past-life regression on myself using Brian Weiss's guided regression and fully experienced my Cliff Palace lifetime.

A couple more words about past life regressions. If you choose to do one, be sure to go into the session with the clear intention that you remember a gentle, happy lifetime for your first trip down past-life memory lane. You really want to make sure you have a good or even great experience for your first time. Also, be sure to write down what you experienced and who showed up in the regression. You will usually find the cast of characters to be familiar. Many of them will be in your current lifetime. As you jot down what you saw and experienced, be sure to open yourself up to filling in the texture of what you experienced. You will discover there is much more information downloaded than you initially thought. Go with the flow without censoring yourself for making all of this up! You may or may not see your death in that lifetime. Again, remember this is not happening at this time, and you can lovingly detach from it.

I would also caution against becoming too enamored of your past lives and forgetting to "be here now." I had had two fabulous past-life regressions that were very empowering, uplifting, and inspiring for me, so I became "hooked" on wanting more and more! The next time I did a past-life regression, however, I found myself ordering the death by drowning of a deformed infant who was one of the people I have had issues with in this lifetime. I completely understood that this was what was customarily done in that situation and the past-life "me" was very matter of fact. The present life "me," however, was absolutely stunned and horrified that I would have done that! It had never occurred to me that I may not have been entirely congruent in my past lives with who I am now! I did discover a reason for a karmic connection that I had with this person, but it also cured me from living in my past lifetimes in a type of spiritual escapism. Please remember that you need to "Be here now!" After all, the only lifetime that you have power over right now is this lifetime. Do not neglect this lifetime while searching for "excuses" in other lifetimes about why your life is not working the way you would like. You are a Divine Being and you have the power to create the life you want by taking congruent action.

CHAPTER 16

Healing

To one degree or another, we are all healers. As Spiritual Beings having a Human Experience, we are much more powerful than we can imagine. It is now the time for anyone who is feeling the call to be a healer to come forward. The Earth herself is going through massive changes and energy shifts as we are birthing a new age of humankind — one where we combine the spiritual aspects of ourselves with our human experience. You will know if you are a healer or a lightworker based upon the things you are attracted to do or read about or are interested in. As a Lightworker it is time, Beloved Warrior of Light, to be impeccable in your life and keep your energy space clear. This means your body – light body, too – and your personal living and working space. It is important to be congruent and learn to speak your truth even if it feels uncomfortable or scary.

There are many types of healing. It is important to truly understand that there is a mind-body connection. Your thoughts, beliefs and feelings create your physical reality. One of the most mind-opening experiences for me, which I mentioned earlier, was when I was recovering from a motorcycle accident. I went to a massage therapist who also did bodywork to release stuck energy in the body. She asked me what unresolved issues I had that caused me to attract this "accident" into my life. I stood there with my mouth open, outraged that anyone would say that my crash was anything but a random accident. It was one of those great "ah-ha" moments for me, but not for a few weeks. I was finally able to see that I truly had attracted this into my life, although if I had been more consciously creating my life, I would have skipped over this one!

Many times, the illnesses that come into our bodies can be healed before they fully manifest in the body. It is much easier to heal toxic thinking and feeling than it is to heal a toxic or diseased body. For example, as I write this, I am reminded of the difficulty of stuffing your feelings in various places in your body. For example, your parents may say that you do not look very good today or you did not do something the way it "should" have been done. You are taught not to talk back, so you store that little hurt somewhere in your body. Eventually your neck feels sore or stiff.

Perhaps your back hurts all the time. Learn to get in touch with your pain to start feeling your feelings and releasing them instead of continuing to store them wherever your body can fit them in!

To keep your body functioning well, energy work is extremely important. Almost, but not quite, as important as the food you eat. So, every day, take your "energetic temperature." Ask yourself, "Where am I emotionally? How do I really feel?"

It is important to find someone who will really listen to you and will not let you hide behind social conventions.

Find at least one spiritual playmate. This will be someone you can be really honest with and truly share the things that are vitally important to you.

Energy healing modalities take many forms. Most typically they take the form of touch. There is healing touch and then more formally, Reiki. Of course, massage is wonderful for healing although it works more on the physical level. Myofascial also works on the physical level, but affects the energy body, too.

I am now doing etheric energy healing that feels as though it really works. Let me tell you my story.

The first person I worked on was a young man named Mason. He went in to have a crown replaced and his teeth cleaned. Things did not go well. He went into toxic shock that caused him to lapse into a coma. My sister knew his mother and she asked for prayers for Mason. Jana Lynne (my sister) asked me to pray for him, so I agreed. When I sat down to pray for Mason, I ended up doing something totally different. I always call in my Guides, Angels and Healers whenever I pray or meditate, and ask for protection and guidance. This time, my guides and angels told me to visualize his body lying on a comfortable table like a massage table. I then started at his head and began to do "virtual" Reiki on Mason. As I did that, I began to receive all sorts of information about him and his condition. I held my hands on his "virtual" body for quite a while and sent him healing energy from God and the Angels. His body really soaked it up. The Angels guided my hands – where to put them and even what color light to send for healing. White Light has all the colors of light anyway, so if you are ever in doubt about what color to use, make it white light. The person or creature (pets/animals) you are working on will use whatever they need. Trust that you are doing the right thing as you put your hands into their energy field.

Mason responded pretty well to the prayers and energy work we all did on him. He seemed to get better for a while although he never came out of the coma. He would rally for a day and then slide down further. We all kept doing healing on him.

The night Mason passed away, his energy body felt and looked different. There was a massive flushing of white light from his feet up to his heart chakra. I did not understand what I was seeing at the time. The bonds his soul had with his body were dissolving. It was beautiful and amazing. It was as if he were much too big to fit into his body anymore. It turns out that was exactly the case and he lovingly returned to Source. Of course, that was devastating for his family, but it was also an amazing, beautiful gift.

What happens when we leave our bodies at the time of death is that all our chakras dissolve and the soul energy flushes out of our crown chakra leaving behind the physical body in a joyous reunion with God/Source. Mason's passing was indeed beautiful, and I was so grateful for all the lessons I learned and for the generosity of his spirit.

Mason allowed me to find an amazing group of Beings who I call the Academy of Healers. They are in the non-physical realm and are delighted to be called upon to help in any healings we feel urged to do. Now (and for quite a while) I call upon The Academy of Healers as well as Archangel Raphael and my team of guides and healers. I then will perform the healing that I described above for the person requesting the healing. I always intuitively knew it worked, but there was no way to quantify it until I started doing chakra readings before the healing and then the next morning. The results have been pretty amazing.

CHAPTER 17

More Tools for Your Toolkit

There are all sorts of additional tools available for your spiritual toolkit if the ones we have talked about so far feel a little too daunting to use. Not to worry! Spiritual tools come in all shapes and sizes and intensities. My deepest desire for you is to find at least one tool that especially resonates with you. I want you to look at each of the descriptions and try any that seem to be attractive to you. Say to yourself, "Well, this one is easy to do for me! I've got this one nailed!" And then go use it or at least try it on to see if it fits!

What are some of these tools? Here are some I have come up with. Be open to finding your own as well.

Dancing, Singing, Connecting with Music...

Dancing or just moving your body to some sort of inspirational music is actually a spiritual tool. Whenever you connect with music whether singing or dancing, you can also connect with your soul. Take some time to play music and dance as if no one is watching! Giggle and be playful. Wear a smile on your face. Did you know that the human body cannot hold onto two emotions at once? When you are depressed, you lower your shoulders, and your face is sad. Typically, your eyes are downcast as well. However, if you choose to then pull your shoulders back and put a huge smile on your face (even if you are faking it), you cannot stay depressed! You must change your state to match your body. Obviously, when you are happy or dancing or singing, you have raised the vibrational frequency of your body, which floods your body with endorphins. So, the next time the world has got you down and beaten you up pretty well, remember to change your body and that in turn will change your feelings and attitude. Lighten Up!

Gratitude Journal...

So often when things aren't going the way we would like we can pout or be grumpy. Unfortunately, if we are vibrating at the level of grumpiness, then that is what we will attract more of. So, to shift our thinking/feeling/doing to a more positive attitude, I have found it helpful to write in a journal about all the things I am grateful for rather than all the bad things that have happened to me. It really helps, although I can certainly tell you there are times that the only things I am grateful for are my dogs and having a roof over my head. Now we are obviously blessed with many other things, not the least of which is our ability to create our own experience. However, sometimes it doesn't seem that way. So, sit down and really identify something you feel good about. Write it down and tell yourself why you are so grateful for this thing. You will start feeling better. The better you feel, the better things you will create in your life.

There is much value in creating new habits, so if you feel like a habit of gratitude is something you want to create in your life, commit to at least 21 days of writing daily in your gratitude journal. I have a friend who actually posts in Face Book daily every November about what she is grateful for in her life. I love how she focuses on the wonderful things that happen in her life rather than thinking about "Oh poor me! Nothing is going right!" So much more empowering for her AND everyone around her. Remember, none of us lives in a vacuum, so what we do for ourselves affects those around us as well.

Books, Bookstores, and your own Bookshelves...

Books have always been one of my biggest joys and sources of inspiration and learning. Especially in the Spiritual World. There haven't always been a lot of classes available to learn these kinds of things, so the brave souls/teachers who are willing to stick their necks out and write about their spiritual experiences have really helped me along my path. I am so incredibly grateful for all of them. Often, there are books that have the exact information you need but you don't know about them. How do you decide which book is right for you at this moment? Always state your intention that you will find whatever is for your highest and greatest good for your own personal growth and development.

A technique I developed for myself was to go into a bookstore (or even browse my own bookshelves) with the intention of receiving guidance from my angels and guides to help me with whatever I was struggling with. Sometimes I would just go in with the intention of being open to a message or a new concept. What you will find is that there will be certain books that will attract your attention. In fact, they almost feel like they are about ready to leap off the bookshelf, or they seem really bright. I would then pick up the book and look through it very briefly. If it resonated with me, I would buy it. If it did not, then I would keep looking. This has been an amazingly effective technique for me.

Messages from Books...

Along the same lines as looking in a bookstore for messages from my guides and angels, I found that I could find specific messages in various books. My favorite technique was to get centered and fully in my body and then open a spiritual book randomly after asking for the highest and best message for me. It was amazing.

It was also very similar to giving myself an angel-card reading or an oracle-card reading. However, if you like this method, there is usually more information on the pages of books than on the cards, even with the little booklet that comes with it.

Do not be afraid to find your messages wherever they may come from. Remember that you are a Divine Being and are powerful, loved & protected.

Love...

Whenever you are feeling love, whether it is for a person, pet, nature, God, the weather, your house, etc., you are vibrating at the very highest level. You are literally made up of millions of atoms and molecules that all have a characteristic vibrational frequency. In addition, your soul, which is the "real" you, also has a specific frequency. The frequency increases when you feel love! When you feel love, everything you see, feel, hear, taste, or touch is better! Do whatever it takes every single day to remind yourself to feel love and gratitude. It does not matter what you do to start the ball rolling. Just find something or someone to love and appreciate. Allow yourself to consciously drop into your heart and feel it open to an amazing outpouring of love. Feel love and appreciation and gratitude for everything and everyone you possibly can. And then feel some more. And more. Build on your mountain of love. See how your day goes then!

Driving alone in your car...

So often when we are driving, we work to distract ourselves by listening to music or books on CD or an audio course. Try this instead, on the highway. Don't listen to anything. Be alone with your thoughts. It is usually helpful if you have a recorder of some sort so you can take a few notes as you are divinely inspired, for that will truly come. It may take a little time, because your mind wants to be entertained. Usually, your mind will finally be lulled by the driving so that your unconscious mind can come out to play and your conscious mind will just let it. This is somewhat akin to meditation as well.

Being out in nature...

Reconnecting to nature just by going out for a lovely walk or bike ride can really clear out the cobwebs in your life and in your thinking. Don't discount that just a little bit of fresh air and a break can revitalize your whole being. In fact, I sometimes call a long walk or bike ride my attitude adjustment, or a moving meditation. As in driving long distances, you can quiet your rational mind and let the divine messages come through.

Crystals...

Crystals are great spiritual tools. Yes, crystals. As you are already aware, your body vibrates with a characteristic frequency unique to you. Crystals also do. If you are attracted to them, they may be an excellent tool for your spiritual journey. I have found that the right crystal can completely shift the energy around you — whether it be in a room, your house or your own personal aura/energy field. By now you should be more aware of your intuition and trust it more than you ever have before. So, follow your internal guidance system in picking out a crystal or crystals for yourself. There is a fabulous crystal store in Albuquerque called Mama's Minerals. I love to go there on a regular basis. However, if you are highly sensitive, I have a bit of advice for your first visit to any crystal shop. Be sure to ground and center yourself before walking into the store. The first time I went in, I was open and extremely excited to feel and see what I could. Within seconds, I became dizzy and felt high as a kite! I had to physically walk out of the store, take a few deep breaths, ground my energy, and then walk back in. Quite an eye-opening experience for me.

Picking out a crystal is fun. Be sure to be open, but grounded. Then pay attention to the direction you feel led. You will find that some things will attract you more than others. This is a deeply private and personal selection time. It is advisable to go by yourself. Otherwise, it may be too distracting for you to properly focus on feeling what you need to feel. Be open to what has called you to the store in the first place. Do not judge whether or not you are picking the right crystal, just open yourself and feel how it resonates with you. You may find you are attracted to a pendant, a sphere, a pendulum, a bracelet, or a large crystal. You will not necessarily know what called you until you get that little chill or excited feeling in your body! The signs are frequently subtle. Do not over-analyze it. If you are in doubt, carry it around for a few minutes as you walk around the store. Once you have decided upon the crystal you really resonate with, be sure to cleanse it once you get it home. I like to do a couple of things. I like to sprinkle it with kosher salt (which, of course, has been blessed) and then rinse it off under a stream of water. I will then frequently Reiki it so that it is infused with my energy and is attuned to me. It will then let you know where it wants to be. Do not argue, even if you have a different spot in mind. Just go with the flow. Your Angels and new crystal will know where the best location for it will be. Trust and believe.

CHAPTER 18

Your Owner's Manual

It is so easy to wander through life not knowing what to do – what is best for each of us. I think all of us have been in this position. I know I certainly did a lot of spiritual seeking, wanting to know what my life's purpose was/is. What a huge burden for us if we feel like we have an assignment here on Earth, but then don't know what the syllabus is or what that life purpose is! Argh! Good news. For the most part, we don't have a specific life purpose. We are here to experience ourselves as a Divine Being in a physical body. Whatever we are deeply drawn to consists of our life's purpose.

When my son was born, I was shocked at how much I really wanted an Owner's Manual for him. What I didn't realize was that we actually DO come with an owners' manual. It's just that we need to learn the language to read it. The language is couched in the subtle feelings we have in our bodies and in our inner knowingness. Unfortunately, this is not taught in school and most of us just wing it. Before you start to beat yourself up for not being able to decipher your own owner's manual, understand that it is an on-the-job training situation. However, it would be nice to have a few tools to cushion the school of hard knocks. That is what this book is all about. It is time you learned for your own unique perspective how you work.

I know I spoke about it earlier in the book, but one of the most eye-opening and transformational things you can do for yourself is to get a Soul Realignment Reading where you will learn what your soul-level gifts or spiritual superpowers are. This is your Owner's Manual.

Your Owner's Manual can also be called your Divine Soul Blueprint. Your soul is made up of eight different energy centers that are similar to but are not chakras. Chakras do not exist if you are not incarnated into a body, but your energy centers always exist. Your soul is made up of bits and pieces of each energy center which added together will total 100%. The energy center which is the largest percentage of your soul is where your primary soul-level gifts lie. This is where you start reading your Owner's Manual. How do you figure out what your primary energy center is? I would highly recommend that you invest in a Soul Realignment Reading to learn what your soul-level gifts are as well as what blocks and restrictions you have created over your current lifetime and your previous lifetimes. It can be beyond transformational for you if that is your path. Only you know what you are led to do in this lifetime.

As far as your soul-level gifts go, there are as many ways to express them as there are people. Each person will have a unique gift with a unique way of looking at the world, which is absolutely perfect. So, the reason for this book is to help you know what some of these spiritual tools are and to create your own toolkit. What fun! Play with this. Enjoy yourself.

CHAPTER 19

Jim's Journey and Transition

Hospitals...

Several years ago, my second husband, Jim LaDue, was hospitalized after an overdose of his medications. I was not allowed to see him even though I was the one who called 911 and helped them get him to the hospital. When I was finally allowed to see him, the energy of the room was awful. There was all sorts of negativity and anger and blame in the room. The nurses and doctors who came through were pretty hateful as well. I was sitting there asking myself what the heck was going on, when it dawned on me that I could shift the energy right then and there. I called on my Guides and Angels and Archangels to clear the energy in that room. To clear the fear energy that was everywhere, but especially in that room. The room had been freezing cold before I did that clearing. Once I did, the room was much calmer and warmed up considerably. Within two minutes I had two different people stick their heads in to see if they could get anything for me. I was shocked at how fast the energy shifted. Jim also improved considerably. His color looked a lot better, and he started breathing much better. It was at that point that it appeared he was going to pull through his overdose. I was stunned at the shift.

You need to know that you have the power to do that as well. It is not just me. I have just had a few more opportunities and situations so that I have the power of belief. Believe in yourself. You really are a Divine Being. Trust in that and go out and live it.

Jim's Transition...

I know it is thought that to take one's own life is a mortal sin, or at least an action that will have consequences. It has been my experience that it depends upon the circumstances. I firmly believe that if you are in great pain and are truly suffering, it may be a total blessing to get a "do over." This is what happened with Jim. He had multiple health issues that just kept piling on until he was beyond miserable. He did not believe he had any power over his own healing process or health. He believed that the doctors would eventually be able to find the magic pill that would heal him. Unfortunately, HE actually needed to be part of the magic pill. He just could not believe that. He had been deeply disillusioned about all things spiritual when he was a teenager. He had followed a guru who ultimately betrayed his followers and showed that he was in it for the money. Jim never got over that, which was his choice of course. Therefore, when he was presented with many different opportunities to heal that aspect of himself, he could not find a way to choose healing for himself.

Ultimately, when he made the decision to transition out of this lifetime, we were finally able to have some very deep and important discussions about spirituality. He was able to receive love and emotional healing, which he had not been able to accept before. His body was simply too damaged to continue, but we were able to find peace and healing between the two of us. One of my mantras is "never leave anything left unsaid." This includes letting the person know how much they are loved and that they are not alone. It also includes forgiving the person for not knowing how to love us back. His passing was, of course, difficult, but also a gentle, loving experience. I know that he was able to move on to his next divine experience. He got his "do over."

CHAPTER 20

More Energy Healing

Reiki or Hands-on Healing...

You are a healer. I know that sounds like quite the statement, but it is true. We all possess the ability to heal others and ourselves. I am reminded of the time-honored healing of our moms or dads when we fall and get a boo-boo! What did they do besides clean the cut and disinfecting it? Most likely they kissed it to make it better. That is actually a form of healing.

Most (if not all of us) want to help anyone who is suffering. The good news is that we can. There are many forms of healing, but primarily all you have to do as a Divine Being is to set your intention that the person or pet to which you are sending energy be healed or helped. The person or pet always has the choice about how to use that energy, by the way, since they are also Divine Beings. Some modalities show that you actually place your hands on the person. Others show that you can do long-distance healing. Both are completely valid. You can do just as effective long-distance healing as in-person healing.

The procedure is very similar for any of the healing modalities. The first thing you do is get centered and breathe. You should be in a quiet, grounded, meditative state. If you are doing healing, then you want to imagine Divine White Light from Source flowing into you from above in through your crown chakra. Feel that White Light fill you up to the point that you are literally filled with joy and happiness and calm. Then allow that Light to flow specifically to your heart chakra. Once there, allow it to flow out through your arms to your hand chakras. This is where the healing energy will flow to your patient or client. If you are doing Reiki or some other modality of hands-on healing, you will actually feel your hands "turn on" and heat up. That is when you place them on the person. In Reiki you hold your hands in the various locations, which actually correspond to chakra points – major and minor—until your feel as though the person has received all the energy they can receive in that location. It is just an intuitive thing. Understand that YOU are not doing the healing. GOD or Source is doing the healing through you, and you are just facilitating where the healing energy is going. Know that you want to be a clear channel and not take on anyone else's pain. It is not for you! You are there to help them flush it out and through their own energy system and body. Many sensitive people are also empaths and will actually take on the pain of their clients or patients. This will limit how many people they can help because they literally are now in pain themselves. No one needs this, least of all the healers who are trying to help.

Healers need to make sure they have good boundaries and need to be crystal-clear that they do not need to take on other people's energies. Refer back to the section about learning to wear your own energy and ONLY your own energy.

Healing...

Our bodies are, of course, energy that is slowed down to seem solid. However, they are still energy. It turns out that most illnesses and diseases are caused by us not being able to bring enough vital force energy through to maintain maximum health. Obviously, there are many factors involved and no one just says, "I am going to create massive disease in my body so I can die painfully through cancer." However, there are energetic markers that can help you see what you need to do to create the best health possible for yourself.

Energy does not lie. We may lie to ourselves about a myriad of things but in the end, if I do a chakra analysis reading for you, I can tell you where you are low and what you need to do to buff yourself up. The chakras metabolize divine energy to animate our bodies. If they are not functioning properly or if they are low in certain areas, then we do not function well. Or not for long.

When we are passing out of this physical experience, our lower chakras start dissolving. They no longer animate the body. In fact, all the chakras dissolve at death. Then your soul can leave the body and go on to its next divine experience.

I have done chakra readings where I determine the percentage of chakra functioning for various people. Obviously, many of these people were ill or feeling terrible or not having any quality of life. One woman I did a chakra analysis for had chakras 1 & 2 that were functioning at 5% and at 8%. Her higher-level chakras were way high. She was literally hallucinating at that point. She was not even functioning. I was able to call in my Academy of Healers as well as Archangel Rafael to help get her back into her body. That worked, but of course, it is only a temporary fix unless she started doing things to ground herself into her body. She did for a while, but she had so many physical situations as well as black mold and methane poisoning that she eventually succumbed. However, we did a lot of other healing before she passed, so I personally believe she has a real leg up on her next incarnation.

CHAPTER 21

Your Spiritual Staff and How to Connect with Them

You are clearly someone who is attracted to or a part of the massive spiritual awakening community, or you would not have even picked up this book. As a spiritually awakened or awakening person, it is critically important for you to really "get" that you are the one co-creating your life with Spirit. So often, many in the spiritual community are waiting for Spirit to tell them what to do. I was certainly guilty of this myself. I was waiting for God or Spirit to send me on my mission or Life's Purpose. All the while, Spirit and my whole team of Guides and Angels were waiting for ME to decide what I wanted to do so they could support me and line things up for me. There is an extremely strict non-interference policy in the angelic and spirit guide world. They cannot tell you what to do or interfere in your life unless it looks like you are about to do away with yourself either accidently or you have somehow put yourself in mortal peril and it is clear that it is not your time to leave your present incarnation. If you want help from your Team of Light, you need to ask for it either directly or by setting your intention that you want to create something in your life. Your Team of Light includes all sorts of beings. Your Team can include Angels, Archangels, Fairies, Spirit Guides, Healers, Ascended Masters and Teachers, Unicorns, Dragons, Dolphins, and any other beings you can think of or imagine. You really are not alone unless you choose to be.

We all have a staff of Angels, Guides and Helpers/Teachers and Departed Loved Ones. I know it sounds like things are a bit crowded around us, but they only step in when we ask them for help. Let's talk about each category.

Angels...

You have as many angels around as you wish. Of course, you have a Guardian Angel who is with you from your birth in this lifetime. Your Guardian Angel's job is to help keep you safe, unless your soul's intention is to experience harm or early death. Remember, you are the boss, so your Higher Self and Soul's intention governs the experience you have. Your Guardian Angel will actually feel like an old friend. Sometimes children have imaginary playmates. Many times, those will actually be their Guardian Angel. They could also be their first position guide, which I will write about shortly.

You can call on your Guardian Angel anytime you want, either aloud or in your mind. They respond to the energy of your request rather than the specific words. We all speak the universal language of love and energy. Once you have called on your angel or angels with a specific request in mind, be sure to take your fingers out of your ears and listen or look for visual clues or inspiration. You will not hear a booming voice telling you what you need to do. Remember, this is all very quiet and subtle. That is why it is so good to employ the various tools in this book.

Spirit Guides...

I have learned so much about Spirit Guides from my education in Soul Realignment, so I would like to share that with you. We are all born with one spirit guide and hire others along the way. These "hirings" typically correspond to developmental times in our lives that are recognized by human development experts. We have an Inner Circle of Guides by the time we are adults that should number 5 or 6. More is not better, and it has been my experience that almost all of us have hired guides to run programs in our energy bodies to act as coping mechanisms for us. These are typically negative or disempowering programs. Obviously, it is better if we have guides all working positively for us, so one of the things that happens during a Soul Realignment Reading is that any coping guides that you hired are thanked for their services and then fired to allow you and your Higher Self to hire all positive guides to round out your team. I have done readings for people who had a guide team of as many as 14 guides, most of which were coping guides running negative programs such as disempowerment or guilt. What a relief for them to get rid of these disempowering programs.

Guides work in the most amazing way. They are souls who have been incarnated before, and thus have a real appreciation for how difficult it can be here on the Earth Plane to create and manifest what we want. Guides understand and are our biggest cheerleaders and helpers. Let me tell you how they may show up in your life. Let's say you are writing an article or a blog and want to reference something your read months ago in one of your books in your own personal library. You cannot for the life of you remember which book it was and don't want to go back through every book. Instead, you gaze at your bookcases and ask which book or books have the information you want to reference in your article. As you soften your gaze, you will find your eye being drawn to a particular book or area of your bookcase. This is your guide team at work. They will actually help you find what it is you need. That is their job, and they are delighted to do it for you. Don't worry about taking up all their time! They are here for you, and they grow, too. They get a front-row seat in witnessing how you navigate your life. One thing the guides are NOT here to do is to tell you WHAT to do. They are here strictly as support staff. If you end up getting the message that your guides are actually telling you to do something, you are not in touch with your guides. You are most likely in touch with a lower level being who is trying to manipulate you. However, you are a Divine Being and you do not ever need to put up with that nonsense! Send them away, then re-center and clear yourself.

Your permanent guide team is a blast to meet once you have fired your coping guides. I am able to introduce you to your team and let you know what each of them looks like and what their role is on your team to help you create the most magnificent human experience possible. It is so nice to know and feel how surrounded by help and love and support you actually are. You are not alone here!

Helpers/Teachers...

These may actually be covered in the Guide Team, but you are free to hire "temps" anytime you wish. These may be in the form of someone who is gifted in writing when you have decided that you want to write a book but would like the words to flow in a more eloquent way. You can literally hire a wordsmith guide to help you. The teachers are also along the same vein. Just as you do not need to keep taking a class from your favorite teacher for the rest of your life, you only need specific help in one area until you have gained a working knowledge or mastery of it. At that time, the Teacher will leave your energy field, but is always available to you should you want a quick "consult."

Departed Loved Ones...

Connecting with your Departed Loved Ones can be a very loving connection but can also be a bit tricky. When one of your loved ones has passed, the initial human reaction is one of loss and wanting to keep them close to you. However, this is not in anyone's best interest. If you hang on to your grandmother who passed over recently, you are actually keeping her from her next divine experience. She is stuck and not able to move on. And you are keeping yourself mired in grief. Believe it or not, you can still keep up the relationship with your grandmother, but make sure she comes back as you call her back, not by you clutching on to her because you do not want to feel grief. Your departed loved ones can come to you in your dreams or even just during the day when you are thinking about them. I know I hear my dad teasing me and calling me "Bethy or Lea Beth" in just the way he used to say that. I also feel great comfort from him when I am feeling down. If I let myself, I can find myself in one of his famous bear hugs where I felt so safe and so loved. Our departed ones are always here for us. We should not tie them down to prevent them from moving on to their next experience.

I had one client who had an attaching soul who turned out to be her ex-mother-in-law, with whom she stayed close even after the divorce. My client was devastated when her ex-mother-in-law passed away unexpectedly. She was really clinging to her and knew that she had an attaching soul. In fact, I had to really work with her to let her know it was the most loving thing she could do to release her mother-in-law. Finally, she did. I also explained to her that she could call on her mother-in-law any time she wanted but could not keep her "stuck" to her. My client reluctantly agreed, and we released her. A couple of weeks later I did a second reading for her which was the Spirit Guide Profile Reading where I introduced her to her permanent guide team for the rest of this incarnation. We were both stunned to find out that the first new guide on her team after firing several negative (AKA Coping) guides was her departed mother-in-law!! I got not only her appearance, but even her name, which she had NOT given me in the previous reading. You can imagine that we both burst into tears of joy and happiness. (As a side bar, this is unusual, but I have now had this happen twice for clients.) Usually, you just talk to your departed loved ones directly whenever you wish.

Sometimes, departed loved ones include our animal companions who have left the physical plane. It can be even more crushing to lose your beloved pet, especially if they have passed much sooner than you think they should have. Obviously, they always leave sooner than we would want them to, but it is especially difficult when they are in the prime of their life and are struck down by cancer or disease. I saw a Facebook post recently showing a person kneeling in front of a gravestone for "Fluffy" and crying. The spirit of "Fluffy" was right behind that person, wagging her tail. This happens quite a bit actually, although our grief keeps us from knowing they are still with us and love us endlessly! We are so blessed to have our beloved animal companions since they show us what unconditional love is in the physical plane.

I did a long-distance healing once on a friend's dog who had a neurological disease and was not doing well. I could tell that was the case but helped infuse the dog with healing energy to use in any way he desired. His mom decided that she could not allow him to continue suffering and did the most loving thing she could do by euthanizing him the next day. A couple of nights later I was doing a channeled writing from my angels when I looked down and saw Monty sitting right next to me just wiggling all over. He was so happy to be free of the pain and the body that was no longer working properly. He was also very clear that he wanted me to let his mom know how much he loved her and how hard he knew it was to let him go instead of putting him through more treatment. He made sure that I would tell her he was around her whenever she wanted to see him and that he would come back to her as another one of her dogs in the future. She just had to let him know when and he would show up for her. He also told me to tell her that if she ever had the feeling that she saw him scoot around the corner, just out of her eyesight, she should rest assured that it was indeed him. I called her either that night or the next morning to let her know and we both had a big cry that was actually very comforting as well. Just know that all of your departed animal companions are still there for you anytime you want. They are sending you love as you read this.

Connecting with your Guides, Angels, or Deceased Loved Ones...

I am frequently asked now how to meet and/or speak to your Angels, Guardian Angel, Spirit Guides or your Deceased loved ones. The primary thing is to be open and willing to hear the messages or to feel them in your body or see something in your mind's eye. The most common way of contacting your Angels and Guides is to simply sit quietly where you will be undisturbed for at least a few minutes. As you allow yourself to slip into a deep, relaxed, quiet state, ask for one of your guides or angels to step forward. You will get an impression of a loving, glowing presence in your vicinity. Do not worry that you do not have a name or recognize specific facial features. If you can feel the energy in some way, rest assured that you have indeed called in one of your Guides and/or Angels. Ask the Angel or Guide to come in a little closer and ask them what their name is. Whatever the first name is that pops into your head is probably the appropriate name for your new Guide or Angel. You may even want to ask what message or gift they have for you. If you are a devoted animal lover, you may find that the guide you have attracted is one of your beloved pets who has crossed over. Or you may find you are in the presence of your favorite grandparent, who is now deceased. Be open and do not discount your impressions by saying, "Oh, I am just making that up!"

When I learned to channel, the process was to meet three guides through a very loving, protected guided meditation and visualization I described earlier in this book.

Once we each met our three guides, we took a break. Channeling takes practice and one must develop "channeling muscles" to hold that energy for a long period of time. When we got back from the break, we asked for the appropriate guide to come through to answer questions from another one of the students. I won't lie – it was scary. I can also tell you that when you are actually channeling, it feels like to your ego you are just making up the answers to the questions. However, it is important to listen to the recording later. You will know that the way you combined the words and how you actually said things, was not exactly how you would have normally said them. Amazing experience. If you get the chance to learn channeling, take it! It is an amazing way to open up your intuition and imagination if nothing else.

CHAPTER 22
More Tools

Journaling... Creating Your Body of Proof...

Unusual things happen to us all the time, but our rational mind will figure out a way to tell us that we are just making stuff up. You are a Divine Being, and you are much more than just this physical body, so it is important to satisfy your rational mind that these things are actually happening. My recommendation is to find a journal of some sort, label it My Spiritual Adventures and be sure to record any and all of the "weird" things that happen to you throughout your days. That way, when your rational mind and ego try to tell you that you are just making this up, you can pull out your journal, read through it and see that this happens quite a bit. I call this your Body of Proof. It is important to actually do this. Even with all of the spiritual "synchronicities" I have had in my life, MY OWN mind will still try to tell me that I am just making it all up. Do yourself a favor if you want to open yourself up to your own Divine spiritual nature — start your journal today. You only need to jot down a few words here and there. Do it!!! Create your own Body of Proof for yourself.

"The What If Game..."

This game comes from the teachings of Abraham, as recorded in the books of Esther and Jerry Hicks. One of the most fun, playful things you can do when you feel like you are stuck in your life and don't know which way to go is to play the "What If Game." This is where you get to use your imagination and pretend your life is a certain way. Every time you feel like you are stuck, say to yourself, "What if I were doing things this other way?" Or "What if I could do anything I want to do in my life, what would that be?" "How would it look?" "What would I be doing?" "How would my life be different from what it is now?" Really play with this. This is also called Creative Visualization.

You cannot create your life on purpose unless you know what it is you want. It's important to spend time daydreaming about what your ideal life might look like. Do not get too attached to the actual form of what this looks like. Leave room for your angels and guides to bring the perfect situation(s) and the perfect people to you. They just may not look quite like what you "imagined" them to look like, so be flexible. One of the things that I always add after I have done one of these visualization sessions is "This or something better."

I have used this game many times in my life in many different areas. Choose any life area that feels most appropriate. In fact, I manifested my amazing life partner (now husband) by using this "what if" game. I had been deeply yearning for a real partner in a romantic relationship. Someone who was spiritual, open-minded, and knew who he was, for the most part, but who was also willing to grow and play. I also wanted someone who was a tennis player (which makes it a bit more specific, but why not?) and who was healthy and active. The wonderful person I manifested into my life showed up too soon and was not really who I was expecting. However, I decided to be open-minded myself and get to know the real person rather than who he presented to the rest of the world. I also realized by doing a past-life regression for myself that we had been together before, but he had died before we were able to be married in that lifetime. That part was quite an eye-opener!

Anyway, the point is that you must give your angels and guides and the universe a little leeway to bring you the essence of what you would like, rather than your very specific and detailed order of what or who you want. There are some who teach manifesting who will tell you to be extremely specific. It doesn't hurt to fill in details but be open your heart's desire not "looking" exactly like what you envisioned. Be open and be willing to spend the time to get to know someone. Don't expect to lock eyes with someone across a crowded room and be done with searching for your life partner.

The same sort of thing can be done with your career, your health, your money, your family, etc. Just remember that you play with the essence of what you want, not exactly what you want.

If you are just wandering through life, then you will just get what you get. Usually, what you get is what others have created for you. Unfortunately, this is not a very satisfying situation. So go play and start creating your life on purpose instead of by default. Stop playing small! You are a Divine Being. Start acting like it!

CHAPTER 23

Ghost Busting...

Property Clearings: Why you need more than smudging...

One more story about house or property clearings. Some dear friends of ours invited us over to dinner, but proudly wanted me to know that they had a ghost in the house. They were actually friendly with the ghost to the point that they had named him Fred. Fred was a bit of a presence in the house, but since I had chosen not to be wide open energetically, he was only a little bit of a nuisance to me. There were a couple of cold spots in the house and spots where the hair on the back of my neck would stand up. Several months later I spoke to my friend about the fact that even though he enjoyed the novelty of having a ghost, this was not actually in the best interest of Fred since Fred was literally stuck in the house! He was not free to go on to his next divine expression and had to get whatever experiences he could by living vicariously through them or any house guests. Fred had a habit of making some electronics work at odd hours of the day or in very strange ways. Finally, my friends (a son and his mother) decided that they should go ahead and have me do a clearing of the house and send Fred on to his next experience. At this point I was able to do the reading and clearing long distance, so that is what I did. I discovered that there was a total of three earthbound souls in the house as well as a portalway to other dimensions and several negative thought-forms in the house. So, I put the clearings into the Akashic Records for the owners to activate with their intention once we had discussed my findings. I asked them to say the following aloud: "It is my intention to activate the clearings and attunement placed into the Akashic Records for this property for now and in all directions of time in all dimensions. And So It Is!" They said they would and hung up the phone. Within 15 minutes, the son called me back and asked me what the heck had I done to the house? It was so very quiet that they could actually turn down the volume on the TV and it felt warmer. We were all very excited that it worked so well. In fact, when I went there for dinner a couple of weeks later, I was amazed at how much "higher" the ceilings felt. All that energetic background noise was gone.

A few months later, another friend was staying at that house. She is a healer and was doing therapeutic massage for the mom and for several other people. She was staying in the bedroom where Fred had always been known to hang out. In the middle of the night, she told me she was awakened by the head of the mattress bouncing up and down by itself rather violently. At least enough to know for sure that she had not dreamt it. So, I went back into the Akashic Records for the house to see what was going on. It turned out that it was still Fred. Somehow, he had been able to refuse to leave. So, I asked him to tell me what the deal was. It turned out that Fred came into the house with the antique bedroom set. He did not want to leave until someone knew who he was and what his story was. So, I listened. He died in that bed of a burst appendix about 100 years ago. He was between 8 and 10 years old and quite the mischievous soul both in life and death. He had strawberry blond hair and freckles. He was particularly drawn to the adult son who lived in the house because he reminded Fred of himself in many ways. Perhaps Fred thought of him as the man he could have become. I then asked Fred if there was anything else he wanted his unwilling hosts to know. He said that he had enjoyed living with them and really appreciated their willingness to "see" him. He also appreciated the fact that I had given them his face and quirkiness. And then he left with a lot of joy and playfulness. I am completely convinced that he will incarnate fairly soon and bring that playfulness to a family situation and really get to express himself.

Even as sensitive as I consider myself to be, it is very difficult to determine everything that is going on energetically in a property unless you ask specifically what is happening. I initially learned to do this through Soul Realignment but have expanded it greatly to allow me to determine very accurately what is going on. For example, I recently went into a business in Santa Fe, where I now live. The business was not open yet and was being built out. My husband and I were chatting with the owners who are friends of ours. I kept shifting around, looking for a comfortable spot to stand. I finally figured out there was something going on energetically that was making me uncomfortable even though I was not sure what it was. After chatting a while, I decided to offer to do a property analysis and clearing as my "housewarming" present to our friends. They agreed. Good thing – they needed it! When I used my pendulum to read the energy of the property by going into its Akashic Records, I learned that it had a Portalway (dimensional doorway), several disruptive earthbound souls, and several negative thought forms. There were even anger spears directed at the property from the previous tenants whose business had failed at that location. I cleared the property, presented my findings to my friends and then had them activate the clearings. This was in the evening. I spoke to my friends the next day and was delighted to hear that they perceived a huge difference in the feel of the property. I did not get a chance to visit the store for a couple of weeks. I was absolutely stunned at the shift in the energy and how good it felt. The interesting thing is that I had been in that store when the previous renters were in it, and I realized that all the things I cleared had been there at that time as well.

The thing I wanted to point out is that for many, many years, I smudged properties and called in Angels to bless and clear them. I know it helped but knowing exactly what you are clearing is massively more effective and powerful.

CHAPTER 24

Connecting with Departed Loved Ones

We all want one last conversation with our departed loved ones. Of course, one way to do it is to find a good, reputable psychic who does mediumship and work with that person. That can be very satisfying, but it can also be very frustrating. Sometimes they get a good, clear message from the other side, but sometimes not so much!! There is another way.

One of the most amazing and empowering things you can do for yourself is to learn to connect with your departed loved ones. It is through the technique called automatic writing. In this scenario, you sit down and center yourself, remembering to breathe in and let out any tension you are carrying when you breathe out. Do this several times. Have a sheet of paper and a pen you love to write with in front of you. When you are ready, write at the top of the paper a loving statement to the person you wish to address. Tell them how much you miss them and how happy you are to know they are now out of pain and in a better place. Ask them if they have a message for you. I usually suggest that you write all of this out. Once you have written your part out, start a new line or paragraph with something along the lines of "My darling (Your Name), I am so happy to have this opportunity to connect with you once again in this way." And then you just write whatever you imagine your departed loved one would like to say to you. I can absolutely promise you that you will feel like you are just totally making up the words that you are writing. All I can say is to keep writing. Go ahead and get everything out that you want to say or that you feel your loved one would like to say. No matter how loud your mind is yelling at you that this is just BS! Then once you are finished, write a note saying how very much you appreciate your loved one for showing up and sharing with you. Then walk away for a while. I have found that you need at least an hour to distance yourself from the writing experience. If you can make yourself wait overnight, that is even better. When you go back and read what has been written, you will realize it is not your voice. You actually channeled a message from your loved one. I know how crazy this sounds and yet I have always been amazed at the messages and deep love that has come through. It is well worth the time spent and no one needs to even know unless you choose to share your experience.

Have fun with this and play with it. As with all tools, however, don't let it take over your life to the point it is interfering with your present life experience. Our lives are meant to be experienced here and now. We can't change the past — but we can certainly affect our future based on the choices we make today in the present. Don't be looking in the rear-view mirror all the time. It's important to look out the windshield and navigate where you want to go.

CHAPTER 25

I See Dead People...

Yes, I know how crazy this sounds, but it's true. I don't actually see a physical body like it was presented in the movie Sixth Sense, but I do see them in my mind's eye. This tends to happen at memorial services or funerals. The first time I was aware of this was at my Stepmother's funeral. I had the most intense feeling of "needing" to get up at the funeral and speak to all the people who were gathered there. I chose not to act upon my impulse, but to this day I am sure that Helen wanted to speak to all the family members who were gathered there to pay their respects. It had been exceedingly difficult for her to communicate in the last few years of her life, so I am sure that she was ready to be heard. I did mention some things that I felt urged to mention after the services to various people. I just didn't really realize it was Helen trying to communicate through me.

One of the next times this happened, one of my tennis friend's elderly mother had passed. I went to the funeral. Again, I had the strongest urge to stand up in front of the family and friends and speak – in a British accent no less! This time, I knew what was going on, so I made a deal with her. I let her know that I would let her channel a written message through me later that evening. I promised I would get the message to her daughter and her two sons. She left me alone for the rest of the services. I sat down that evening and let her write a letter to her children and grandchildren. The funny thing is that I actually could hear her voice while I was writing this letter to the children. I gave it to my friend who was deeply grateful. I also said it was okay to give it to her two brothers as well, since I didn't really know them. Both reached out to me to let me know how much that letter had moved them.

Another time (funeral again) I didn't know the woman who had passed. I knew her daughter, so I went to show support for her. I did not get a message from her, but I looked to my left and saw my Broker (Tony) who had passed away just a couple of months before. He was stretched out in his chair just like he had done when he was in the physical form. And he said "Yo," which was one of his typical sayings. He then said, "Look who I have with me." I looked around him and saw my second husband, Jim, who blew me a kiss. Next to him was another friend's deceased husband. He asked me to let his wife know he was great and to enjoy her life. These three were those who most looked like they were physically there rather than just in my mind's eye. I also frequently "saw" Tony around the office. At one point I asked him if he was stuck or just hanging around. He let me know that he had transitioned just fine but felt like he was wanted to be felt around the office, so he stuck around. It was very comforting to "see" him so vibrant and alive, since his death was devastating to us all.

The moral to this story is to not be afraid of seeing departed loved ones. It can be reassuring that their essence and soul goes on even if their physical body does not.

CHAPTER 26

Heeding the Call to be an Earth Angel

Angels and Guides do not usually materialize out of thin air to hand us the answer to our requests (also known as prayers). They must work through other people or through messages we receive in other ways such as through our computers, an article we read or see on TV. We can even receive the exact answer to our prayers by "accidently overhearing" a conversation being held between two people at the next table! Our prayers are always answered, even a shouted prayer! I want to share with you in a little more depth one of my shouted demands/prayers.

I was in a very dark, heavy situation where I was at the end of my rope. My husband, Jim, was very ill and also in a very dark, angry place. I was very energetically, emotionally, physically, and financially depleted. I was driving to my office, crying, when I finally really yelled at God and the Angels! I said (screamed), "I need your help and I need it now! I have had it and can't do anymore!" I got to my office and did some paperwork and calmed down a bit. I actually sat down in the front of the office, which I never ever did, and chatted with another agent and our office staff for about five minutes. A woman walked into the office and asked for Tony (my Broker). He was out of town. As she was turning to leave, I recognized her even though I hadn't seen her in five or ten years. She was a spiritual nutritionist who I had seen for many appointments who I really loved and connected with. I had admired her boldness and frankness about following and connecting with Spirit. My husband at the time had persuaded me to quit seeing her since he had decided she was a quack. Well, all I can say is thank God she listened to her angels that day because she saved my life and helped clear me so that I could finally find my own connection with God again! I am so grateful that she was willing to be an Earth Angel and deliver my Angel's message to me that they were there for me and were indeed helping me through the dark ordeal I was living through.

I am sure as I write this that Saari was acting upon her inner nudging (or not so subtle nudging) of her angels and guides as well as mine. In fact, one of the most amazing things I heard from her that day was that even though she felt strongly compelled to go see Tony right then, she was clearly there for me, and she wanted me to know that I wasn't alone. She truly was my lifeline that day. She asked me to come to her house the next day and we did a clearing and smudging of me. I was wearing at least two very dark, fear-based entities who were literally choking the life force out of me. I could not feel any connection to God or Love or Light. It took a couple of heavy-duty clearings as well as clearing my house and my husband (who had attracted the dark entities in the first place) so that I was able to finally feel hope and optimism instead of this crushing depression. I was able to feel lighter and connected to God/Source. What a blessing she was in my life! I had always appreciated her and really loved her, but that day she modeled what it was to be an Earth Angel. My definition of an Earth Angel is someone who allows themself to hear/feel/see/know spirit and then act as a conduit or channel to tell someone else what the Angels are nudging them to say to that person. It takes enormous courage to be an Earth Angel since you will be risking (at least in your mind) enormous ridicule from those around you for being "out there" or "woo-woo." So, I must confess that for the longest time, I would receive impressions or nudgings to say something to various people I would run across, and I would keep my mouth firmly shut! As I look back, I can only hope that the messages I didn't deliver got delivered in some other way. Fortunately, I do know that our angels and guides can be extremely creative in the different ways they get messages to us.

Again, one of our jobs is to start being more sensitive and alert to all sorts of messages and avenues of communication. In fact, once you allow yourself to be open to the idea that they are always sending you messages to answer whatever you have asked for or about (prayer), you will be staggered at the number of messages you are getting. You are a Divine Being and are having "psychic" events all the time! There are no accidents!

CHAPTER 27

What Next?

It is my greatest hope that you now have found some spiritual tools for your Spiritual Toolbox that will help you hear directly from God, Source, Angels, Guides, Fairies, Ascended Masters, Departed Loved Ones, Animal Protectors, and anyone else you can think of who is on your Spiritual Staff. Believe in yourself! Remember: You are a Divine Being having a physical experience. You are co-creating your life with Spirit. The little everyday choices you make that are more aligned will create massive changes in your life. Your inner knowingness as well as your direct messages from your staff will help you determine what changes to make to align with who you really are – not who you always thought you were. Make Soul Inspired choices every day and be prepared to create miracles in your life!

So go out and be the best possible version of yourself! You can change the world by changing yourself.

Appendix 1

Chakra Clearing and Healing...

Just a quick reminder that you are a Divine Being having a physical experience. You are MUCH more powerful than you think or have been led to believe. You are actually able to Clear and Re-charge your chakras based upon your own intention and attention. Remember that your chakras allow you to anchor your soul into these wonderful bodies as well as animating your bodies. The better your chakras function, the better and more vibrant your health. You are recharging your body with Vital Force Energy.

Our Chakras are very complex, but for the purposes of this meditation, we will look at chakras as being spinning crystal balls. This viewpoint is actually profoundly effective and healing. Trust the process.

When you do this meditation, be sure to get into a nice, comfortable seated position. Yes, you may do this laying down as well, but I personally tend to fall asleep before the clearing is done if I do that, so I recommend a seated position. Close your eyes and begin to follow your breath. Imagine your consciousness flowing into your body as you inhale and then flow out of your body with the exhale.

At this point, call in the presence of 100,000 angels to heal and protect you during this process. Know that they are there once you request their help even if you think you are just making this all up (or that I am!!!).

Once you are calm, centered, grounded, and protected, you will want to start the actual clearing and healing process.

Here is a quick summary of the process:

You will look at each chakra with your mind's eye and do a quick "examination" of the chakra. Here are some of the things to "look" for.

1. Is the chakra you are looking at cloudy or muddy looking?
2. Are there dark spots in the chakra?
3. Is the color off? Is it too dark or too bright? Does it seem washed out?
4. Is it spinning? Or is it stationary or static?

Once you have determined the state of the particular chakra you are looking at, call on your angels to bring in the correct color of that chakra. Ask your angels to infuse the chakra with light, love, and healing. Ask that they keep sending light to that chakra until it is like a clear crystal (in the color it should be) without any dark spots and is spinning in a clockwise direction if you were looking at it from the viewpoint of standing in front of your own body. This clockwise direction will allow you to metabolize Vital Force Energy!

Then move on to the next chakra and go through the same process until you have gone through all 7 primary embodied chakras. In addition to the 7 in our bodies, we have another 5 that are becoming increasingly important as we go through the ascension process, so I am including those as well.

Going through each chakra:

1ˢᵗ Chakra: Your 1ˢᵗ chakra is called your root chakra and is located at the base of your spine. This chakra affects your ability to connect to tribe, family, and society. Its color should be a vibrant, deep, ruby red. Remember to call on your angels to make sure it is fully functional and a perfect color and clarity. It should also be spinning in a clockwise direction. Stay here and keep your attention on this chakra until you "know" it is exactly the right color and clarity. Then move on to the next chakra.

2ⁿᵈ Chakra: Your 2ⁿᵈ chakra is called your sacral chakra and is located below your navel. This chakra affects your money and sexuality as well as confidence, emotional balance, manifestation and vitality. Its color should be a gorgeous, orange color. It should be the color of a perfectly ripe orange picked straight from the tree. If it is not that vibrant color or exhibits cloudiness or murkiness or dark spots, again call on your angels to bring in a fabulous orange healing light to bring that chakra to the color, clarity, and rotation it should have to be fully healed and recharged. Stay with it until you "see" it so in your mind's eye. Once it is, move on up to the next chakra.

3ʳᵈ Chakra: Your 3ʳᵈ chakra is called your solar plexus chakra and is located above your navel – literally where your physical solar plexus is. This chakra affects your self-esteem and personal goals as well as your center of power and strength. It is the color of a beautiful, ripe lemon. It should be vibrant and sending out a lovely yellow light. If it is not, based on your observation, then call on your healing angels again to bring that chakra up to fully healed and functional. Keep up that process until you clearly "see" it healed.

4ᵗʰ Chakra: Your 4ᵗʰ chakra is called your heart chakra and is in the middle of your body rather than to the left where your physical heart is located. It is your center for relationships with yourself and others. It is also the transition between your physical body chakras and your spiritual/upper-level chakras. It is the color of the most amazing perfect green emerald. It is spectacular. Some people see it as pink rather than green. If it feels more correct to you to visualize it as pink, then do so! Either will work. So often we are quite wounded in our heart chakra, so be sure to spend time on this chakra until it feels greatly expanded and sending out love to the world and the people around you. Again, look for the color and clarity of the chakra before you move on to the next one.

5th Chakra: Your 5th chakra is called your throat chakra and is located at your throat. This is the center of communication and self-expression. This particularly important chakra is what allows you to express your own authentic viewpoint and creativity. It is the color of a robin's egg blue or an aquamarine or turquoise. Look at yours and diagnose whether it is functioning properly. If it is not, call on your healing angels to take care of that. Stay with it until it is that gorgeous aquamarine color.

6th Chakra: Your 6th chakra is your third-eye chakra and is located between and slightly above your physical eyes. It is the center for intuition, vision, imagination, and truth. It is the color indigo which is a combination of purple and blue. It is quite the "royal" color. Make sure that it is spinning as well as being the crystal color of vibrant indigo.

7th Chakra: This is the last of the 7 major embodied chakras. It is called your crown chakra and is located at the top of your head (crown). It is the center of personal freedom and ability to choose. It is also the center of wisdom and connection to your higher powers. It is a gorgeous violet color when functioning at its optimal level. Be sure to spend time on this chakra to clear and heal it. When this chakra is functioning correctly, you will have the freedom to create your life in the highest and most aligned way possible.

The next set of chakras...

8th Chakra: This chakra is about a foot above the top of your head and is called the Soul Star Chakra (names may vary). I see it as a silvery color. This chakra is where you connect with your Higher Self and the conduit to connect with spirit. In addition, it is the center of common sense and rational thought. Be sure it is spinning and clear before you move on to the next chakra.

9th Chakra: This chakra is located about 18" above the top of your head. It is frequently called the Spirit Star Chakra and is the center for Spiritual Wisdom. I see this one as a silvery white color. If you are tapping into your Spirit Star Chakra, you will simply tap into the wisdom of the Universal Consciousness. This chakra and the additional ones above it typically do not need clearing but look at it anyway with your intuition to see if there is anything off.

10th Chakra: This is your Universal Chakra and is your connection with Pure Consciousness. It is also pure white. It is located 5 – 6 feet above your head.

11th Chakra: This is called your Galactic Chakra, and it connects you to your own Divine Knowledge. I see it as a beautiful golden-tinted white light.

12th Chakra: This chakra is called your Divine Gateway Chakra and is the connection to Universal Consciousness. I see this one as a brilliant Golden Color.

0th Chakra: In addition to your higher-level chakras that are part of your energy field, but not in your physical body there is one more chakra. I have designated it as the "0" Chakra. It is also called the Earth Star Chakra. All our chakras are extremely important, but this one is especially important for our physical incarnation. We are Divine Beings (souls) currently having a physical body. It is critical for our sense of well-being, safety, and health that we be deeply rooted or grounded into Mother Earth. This is the function of the Earth Star Chakra. To ground yourself into your physical body, simply imagine yourself sending out energetic roots out the bottoms of your feet down into Mother Earth. Feel how nourished and safe you feel once you are fully rooted.

Remember, a tree can only grow as tall as its root system is deep. The better grounded you are, the higher the levels you can reach spiritually.

Final Cleansing/Clearing:

Once you have cleared your chakras with this method, sit quietly for a few more moments while you call in Divine White Light to finish your clearing. Visualize this like a beautiful shower of White Light that washes your chakras, aura, and other energy bodies with cleansing and healing energy. See any impurities or entities gently and lovingly washed away and taken to the Divine for purification.

Feel how much calmer, quieter, and lighter your body feels. You can do this meditation anytime you have just a few minutes. In fact, many times you can just skip to the shower of White Light if you have cleared your chakras recently. White Light has ALL the colors in it, so you automatically recharge your chakras with just that.

Be sure to thank your angels who came in to heal and protect you. Then thank yourself for showing up to do the clearing.

www.ingramcontent.com/pod-product-compliance
Lightning Source LLC
LaVergne TN
LVHW051843080426
835512LV00018B/3044